LOVE
IN THE TIME
OF COLIC

LOVE
IN THE TIME
OF COLIC

THE NEW PARENTS'
GUIDE TO **GETTING**
IT ON AGAIN

Ian Kerner, Ph.D., and Heidi Raykeil

This book contains advice and information relating to sexual health and inter-personal well-being. It is not intended to replace medical or psychotherapeutic advice and should be used to supplement rather than replace regular care by your doctor or mental health professional. While all efforts have been made to assure the accuracy of information contained in this book as of the date of pub-lication, the publisher and author are not responsible for any adverse effects or consequences that may occur as a result of applying the methods suggested in this book. All names and biographical details of patients and participants have been modified to protect their confidentiality. In some cases, stories have been combined to create a composite that helps illustrate a point.

LOVE IN THE TIME OF COLIC. Copyright © 2009 by Kerner-Rubisch, Inc., and Heidi Raykeil. All rights reserved. Printed in the United States of America. No part of this book may be used or reproduced in any manner whatsoever without written permission except in the case of brief quotations embodied in critical articles and reviews. For information, address HarperCollins Publishers, 10 East 53rd Street, New York, NY 10022.

HarperCollins books may be purchased for educational, business, or sales promotional use. For information, please write: Special Markets Department, HarperCollins Publishers, 10 East 53rd Street, New York, NY 10022.

FIRST EDITION

Designed by Susan Yang

Library of Congress Cataloging-in-Publication Data
Kerner, Ian.
    Love in the time of colic : the new parents' guide to getting it on
again / Ian Kerner and Heidi Raykeil.
        p. cm.
    ISBN 978-0-06-146512-3
    1. Sex in marriage.   2. Husband and wife.   3. Sexual excitement.
    4. Childbirth.   5. Infants.   I. Raykeil, Heidi.   II. Title.
    HQ21.K277 2009
    613.9'608655—dc22
                                                    2008027523

09 10 11 12 13   OV/RRD   10 9 8 7 6 5 4 3 2 1

For Lisa and JB,

and our beautiful children

who make it so hard . . . and so worth it.

Contents

LOVE
IN THE TIME
OF COLIC

Welcome to the Jungle

LIGHTS, CAMERA . . . ACTION?

Picture this: Mom and Dad crawl into bed after finally getting the baby to sleep. For the moment, the little one is in the crib, and as much as they'd like to believe he'll stay that way, they know it's only a matter of time. For Mom's part, she just wants to read a few sentences of the same paragraph of the same novel she's been mulling over and over and then close her eyes and snatch a few moments of precious sleep.

Dad, meanwhile, has other plans: He sidles on over, gently pushes away the novel, and presses his body (and hard-on) against her. *You've got to be kidding me*, she thinks to herself. *How can he even think of sex? There's no way this is going to happen.*

But tonight he's determined; he won't take her subtle back-turn as an answer. He knows he has a tiny window of time and has to act fast; maybe, just maybe, he'll get some action: charity sex, a blow job, even a hand job. Hell, at this point anything other than his own hand would do. So she kisses him back, at first out of a sense of obligation. But soon, as she starts to remember long lost grown-up sensations, she does it because (what's this?) she kind of wants to! The force of his hunger puts her in touch with appetites of her own. (Maybe this guy isn't so bad after all.) For a few precious moments they are back to being a couple—not just co-parents—with no thoughts other than each other. There is no world outside of this bedroom, no world outside of their touch.

Until the crying begins.

Although Dad has purposefully turned down the baby monitor (a cheap ploy, he knows), the wails reverberate through the walls. He continues to kiss and grope, urging her to let the baby cry—it's okay if he cries a little, he tries to reason, knowing in his gut it's already a lost cause. And then he prays: *Please, please, please go back to sleep. For Pete's sake, sleep.*

But it's already a fait accompli for Mom. Her whole body pulls toward the baby, her whole being is affected by his tiny little cries. She rushes up, throws on some old sweats, and soon returns to bed, cooing over the breathless baby latched to her breast. Dad knows his chance is shot. He turns away and faces the wall. Whereas minutes ago they were deeply connected, they are now a million miles apart.

Don't be angry, she wants to say; it won't always be like this. She reaches out to him, but he recoils at the touch, springs from the bed, and leaves the room, silently. From the bedroom, she hears him pacing and muttering under his breath. She doesn't know whether to cry or curse him out.

Welcome to the jungle. Welcome to love in the time of colic.

Thanks to Carrie Bradshaw and company, our generation is now comfortable laughing about the big O over cosmos—and thanks to our modern metrosexual husbands, we can equally share diaper duty and hair creme. But as swinging and savvy as new parents are today, there's still one very old-fashioned topic we just don't know how to talk about: Sex. After. Baby.

These three words are spoken in hushed voices over playdates and at playgrounds by mothers and fathers everywhere, stumped and shocked by the state of their sex lives. For a generation inculcated with individualism and weaned on sexual empowerment, we're as surprised as anyone when our sex lives end up stale. But while we may whisper about it to our closest girlfriends, or make jokes after one too many beers with the guys, when it comes to talking with our partners about what's really going on (or not going on, as the case may be) in our baby-proofed bedrooms, more and more of us find ourselves tongue-tied and tiptoeing. Authors included. When it comes to not getting it on, we've been there, done that, and found our way back to doing it more.

IAN'S STORY: "HOP ON POP . . . PLEASE!"

If parenthood has taught me one thing it's that, irrespective of my public persona as a relationship expert, I am far from being an expert in my own relationship. Like many a new father, life after baby #1 left me confused and conflicted, not to mention sleepless, sexless, hard up, and horny. And just when I thought I couldn't get any hornier, along came baby #2 to take my horniness to new dimensions of dementia. There was a point when everything made me think of sex. One time my wife, Lisa, was reading the Dr. Seuss classic *Hop on Pop* to our then toddler, Owen, and I found myself thinking, "Hey Lisa, why don't you come over here and hop on this pop?" This is a pop who could use some hopping!

Let me tell you: When even Dr. Seuss makes you think of sex, that's when things have to change.

And this book is indeed about change—the changes that parenthood wreaks on your sex life, and how to adapt and master those changes without letting them masturbate . . . I mean, master you. As you can see, I may be a sex therapist, but I'm first and foremost a guy and I've grappled, and continue to grapple, with these issues: interminable nights with all four of us squeezed into the bed; feeling sex-starved and pissed off; tuning out, turning off, and becoming prey to all the pitfalls that go along with that vulnerable state. As far as I'm concerned, there are no quick fixes, no thirty-day plans for change, no clinical psychobabble —all I can promise is honesty, knowledge, experience, not to mention a guy's perspective, as well as some tools and tricks to help you through the long day's journey into night.

I'm ashamed to say it, but the truth is that on more than one night (way more than one night, actually), I've been that angry guy in the scene described earlier. The changes parenthood wrought on my sex life left me feeling rejected, dejected, angry, and spiteful. But instead of rising to the occasion and stepping up to the plate as a husband and father, I acted like an asshole, which is all the more ironic (and assholey) because if anyone should know better it's me!

Heidi and I have joked that we should have called this book *What to Expect When He's Expecting Sex*, except that would have left us open to criticism and a lawsuit for trademark infringement. Looking back, it wasn't that what I wanted from my wife—sex—was wrong. In fact, clinical experience has shown me that in "expecting sex" the new father is often performing a vital relationship function, which is to bring his partner back into the relationship and restore the primacy of their couple-hood—a crucial necessity if they're to flourish and succeed as a family.

What I wanted wasn't wrong, but how I was going about it was beyond the pale. I guess it's not always easy, especially when you're in the thick of it.

In her book, *Confessions of a Naughty Mommy*, Heidi writes, "No one warned me that having a baby was like the excitement of falling in love all over again, except with someone much younger and better smelling than my husband. No one told me that for all intents and purposes, having a baby was dangerously similar to having an affair."

In retrospect, I can see that I was acting like a spurned lover and kicking up a shit-storm along the way. I was not only competing at the same volume as the "other man" in my wife's life (in this case an infant), but I could one-up him with meanness and mind-games. In losing my wife to this little creature, I felt like the rug had been pulled out from under me. I wasn't just "not getting it on," I was angry as hell, too!

So what was I really expecting in expecting sex? Not just blow jobs and orgasms (although those are always nice), but the intimacy and sense of connection that is part and parcel of a healthy sex life.

Not too long ago I was on a plane with my kids, and I thought I better take some time to really listen to those pre-flight instructions about safety exits and flotation cushions that I normally ignore. And I was profoundly struck by a simple instruction: "In the event an oxygen masks drop down, put it on yourself first, then your children." They instruct you to do this because you have to take care of yourself to take care of your kids. Well, in our marriages we're constantly putting our children first, to the point where we allow our relationships to suffocate in the end, everyone ends up suffering for lack of air. This book is about getting the oxygen mask on and taking a deep breath. As an individual. As a couple. As a family.

HEIDI'S STORY: IT'S THE END OF THE WORLD AS WE KNOW IT . . . AND I FEEL FINE

Ten years ago, before kids and mortgages and All That, my husband JB and I were experts in the language of love. If sex is a form communication, well, back then we were on the un-limited calling plan. We may not have always talked explicitly about the details, but we never had trouble communicating, we never had trouble connecting, physically or emotionally. And then . . . we had a baby. And while in some ways our daughter's birth brought us closer together than ever, in other ways (like actually having sex or even talking about it) we grew apart.

Worse than trying to figure out the logistics of post-baby sex was trying to figure out what had happened to my once level libido. Ian, true rockin' animal that he is, confided to me that if his experience with sex after baby had a theme song it would be Guns N' Roses' "Welcome to the Jungle." That's the truth. But in my "not getting it on" world after baby, I think my theme song would have been another '80s hit—"It's the End of the World As We Know It (And I Feel Fine)." Although I missed wanting sex, I didn't actually miss having sex. I felt fine without it! And I had no idea how to explain that to my husband. How could I? I didn't know what was happening myself. Before long, my husband and I created a whole new way of communicating about sex—one that used very few of those pesky, um, words—and instead used plenty of late-night fights. Bye-bye language of love, bye-bye unlimited calling plan. Hello pre-paid calling cards with desperately low minutes.

Those early years after the birth of our daughter were tough; there were times I was afraid to accidentally brush against my husband's foot at night because I thought it would give him the wrong message. There were times I saw his erect penis as a little drill sergeant: Hup, two, three, four / I am just another chore. There were times I wanted nothing more than to be left alone with my beautiful baby and a clean house. But finally, after four years, another baby, and writing a book on the topic, I think I know a little more about what was really going on. I can now see the pitfalls and traps of the baby sex jungle. I know I get caught up into giving too much to others, I know I need regular exercise, I know I've got a funky thyroid. I know I tend to throw myself into motherhood as an excuse for not looking at my own life sometimes. I know I fall in love with babies, hard. My husband and I also now know how to explain our feelings about all this without attacking, blaming, or denying.

People are always asking me what's the number one thing they can do to (start wanting to) get it on again. I joke that they should write a book about it! But I'm only half joking, because it was through writing about it that JB and I starting talking about it. Really talking about sex and work and parenting and how hard it is to make it all function. As it turns out, talking about sex (or the lack of it) doesn't take away the magic—it's darn near the only thing that really makes it happen. Thanks to our (now endless) discussions, JB now also knows he's my real number one, even when I am in the harpylike throes of intimacy overload. He knows that eventually the baby who has displaced him will wean and sleep and one day even walk away from us. He also knows that, intimacy junkie that I am, I will turn once again to him to get it. I hope this book can do the same for you—I hope it can get you talking, and turning, once again to each other.

YOUR STORY: WHY YOU'RE READING THIS BOOK

Just as becoming a parent changes who you are, it also undoubtedly changes your sex life. After all, committed relationships are built on predictability, dependability, and accessibility, whereas let's face it: Sexual attraction is often about spontaneity, unpredictability, mystery, and danger. And it's pretty hard to be all mysterious and unpredictable in between scheduling playdates and mommy-and-me classes.

Building sexual anticipation—a key to getting that wanting part back—is hard enough in any long-term relationship, but when you throw kids in the mix, it really can brew up some serious trouble. Let us reassure you—you're not the only ones. While we both came from this topic from very different places, it's clear to us that sex after baby is still a subject that people navigate like a minefield. In his practice, Ian comes across couples struggling to get "the magic" back—or get any magic at all. Heidi still gets letters from moms across the country who read her book and want to share their relief at the realization that they are not the only ones going through this. It's also a reality we're both still living, every day, even as we write this. We're dimpled-knee-deep in this too. Throughout the book we'll continue to share our own personal stories with you, as well as give it our best shot to speak, and spark debate, on behalf of men and women everywhere who are living and loving in the time of colic.

Here are some signs you're a part of this unfortunate "club":

- You ask your ob-gyn for "another six weeks of freedom"
- The mind-blowing sex you used to have now just blows
- The TV is turned on more than you are
- You *want* to *want* sex, you just . . . don't
- You'd rather go on a playdate than another bad date night
- The baby gets way more kisses and cuddles than you do
- You're beaten down (and beating off) from always having to initiate sex
- You have a user ID like "sexydad" or "hungrymama1"
- Foreplay has become chore-play
- "Let's get it on" are now fighting words
- You'd rather sleep than sleep with your partner

Sound familiar? Don't panic—you don't have to throw out the post-baby sex with the dirty bathwater. The good news is, because we've been there ourselves we won't try to sell you a bill of goods we all know isn't true; we both agree we can't give you a quick seven-step program or promise great sex in just ten days. But by joining us, you've taken the first real step in making it right. You've started a lifelong conversation about sex and long-term love and how to keep that from becoming an oxymoron. And while we can't give you a magic cure, we can share our experience with you, and give you some strategies and skills to help you alleviate your acute symptoms of "parent-no-sex-itus" and offer some long-term prevention. We can get you communicating and connecting again, even if you're not always agreeing.

IT'S NOT ALL FUN AND GAMES

Although we've purposely kept the tone of this book light and breezy and fun, the truth is, as we like to say here in Parentland, *it's not all fun and games*. What we're really asking you to do is take a good hard (hopefully!) look at yourself and your partner—to actively participate in the exercises and open this seriously sexless can of worms. Yes, it takes courage and strength to go there with us, but it's worth it. As you read this book, you'll learn what pitfalls to watch out for, what you can do to get sex going again, and hopefully a little about yourself and each other that you didn't know before.

Does one size fit all? Of course not. Our general format of Heidi speaking for the moms and Ian speaking for the dads allows for some sharing of personal experiences and plenty of spirited back and forth. But we know it's a lot more complicated than just he said/she said. After all, sex after baby (or no sex after baby) is often an equal opportunity bummer. And while a fair portion of this book assumes that it's the male partner who is sex-starved, plenty of couples find themselves dealing with the opposite. Other couples might not include any men or any women in them at all! We wrote this book based on some generalizations from what we've learned in our own lives and work. That means it may not fit you exactly. But it is a place to get things started, a way to bring up topics we too often avoid looking at, the ones we too often brush under the rug and out of the way—until one day, whoops, we trip.

HOW TO USE THIS BOOK

Because we know you're sleepless, sexless, hard up, and horny, we know that time for reading can be difficult to find. So feel free to jump right in with this cheat sheet:

- *Brand new baby?* Want that "get out of sex free" card? We won't give it to you, but in Chapter 1 we will give you some tips for jump-starting things . . . without too much backfire.
- *Colicky baby?* No, despite our clever title, we don't have specific tips for this. But we do know that babies with special needs can equal parents with unmet needs of their own. For that reason we recommend grabbing your partner and diving right in. The between-chapter diagnostics are a good place for you to see where you're at now and where you'd like to go.
- *In a hurry for some practical tips?* Gloss over the main parts of each chapter and skip to the Sex RX at the end of each chapter. It's just what the doctor ordered for getting your groove back.

- *Got the third-wheel blues?* The baby blues? Some other shade of blue? Fill up with a little support pit stop in Chapter 2.
- *Would you rather do the dishes than your partner?* Is sex just another job on a long to-do list? Then push Chapter 3 to the top of yours.
- *Dad, do you get up at night more easily than you get it up?* Mom, still hoping your maternity pants will come back in fashion? Do the words "let's get physical" make either of you think about how tired, out of shape, and generally yucky you feel? You're not alone, and Chapter 4 can offer some real succor. (Guys, we said succor, not sucking.)
- *Has date night become hate night?* Grab your honey, grab this book, and go read Chapter 5 at a café over a glass of wine. Or skip to the Mini Sex RXs throughout the chapter for instant date-night assignments.
- *Does sex just not rock your boat anymore?* Maybe it never gave you the motion of the ocean you wanted or the excitement in bed has just died way down. Chapter 6, with tips for shaking things up a bit, will have you screaming "land, ho" in no time.
- *Do you feel like the loss of connection is getting really serious?* We know that you're real and human and we're going to treat you that way. Shit happens in your sex life. Porn, infidelity, slumps that go on and on. And kids make this all the harder. So if you're a real person with

some real problems, do not pass go and head straight
for Chapter 7.

In this time of colic, it can feel like you're headed for a lifetime of not getting it on. Our belief and experience say otherwise. We think you can get this jungle swinging once again.
We think—no, *we know*—it really is possible to do the hokeypokey and keep up the hanky-panky. Or to read *Hop on Pop*,
and then actually want to hop on pop. While we may reach
this conclusion from very different perspectives at times,
what we both agree on is that *sex matters . . . a lot*. Parents can
give their children everything, but nothing is a substitute for
parental happiness. And in our opinion, sex is the glue that
holds couples together and keeps lovers from simply becoming roommates or co-parents. So here we are to help you keep
things fluid out there, to take the charge out this once taboo
issue, and put the charge back where it should be—in the
bedroom.

CHAPTER ONE

Back in the Saddle Again: Why It's So Darn Hard to Start Having Sex Again After Having a Baby

LIGHTS, CAMERA . . . ACTION?

Picture this: A new mom returns from her six-week postpartum checkup to find several messages from her husband who is eagerly awaiting the news. All clear for takeoff? All systems go? Are we romance-ready? He certainly is, and that night, after the baby is asleep, he makes his move. Mom tries to get into it, but her boobs are heavy and full, she's self-conscious about her body, and none of her husband's standard techniques are getting her excited. He can sense her hesitation and pulls back a little, afraid of getting to the point of no return and, well, having to return. She doesn't know how to take his sudden lack of "liftoff," so she pulls back too. It's a series of misconnections and misfires. Even as they begin to make love, neither is really present; the result is unromantic, uncomfortable fumbling. In the anti-afterglow, Mom rushes up to check on the baby, while Dad lies in bed, unsure about what just happened. "Houston, we have a problem."

HEIDI: *Yikes—space travel metaphors aside, that scenario sounds a little too familiar. Here's what I really want to know—who came up with this whole six-week number anyway? Clearly it's some kind of conspiracy, fueled by male gynecologists.*

IAN: *Maybe so—but you know it's not all get up and go from the male side either—we've seen a lot over the past nine months, maybe a little too much if you know what I mean . . . last we saw, in the delivery room, it was pretty Apocalypse Now/Heart of Darkness down there. . . .*

HEIDI: *Try living it!*

IAN: *Touché.*

HEIDI: *You know, it would actually be easier if this whole "saddle shy" issue were only a result of the changes in those weeks after childbirth. But you and I both know all too well that what starts out as a little slump can quickly become a serious rut.*

IAN: *That's right. According to a recent CNN report, more than 40 million Americans are stuck in a sex rut, and I bet many of those slumps followed the birth of a child. So regardless of where you are in the "sleepless, sexless, hard up, and horny" timeline, whether it's six weeks, six months, or even six years, it's time to get the ball rolling again.*

So here you are. You've bought the condoms (you better have!), you've shaved your legs. (Maybe. Armpits at least?) But now what? In some ways it was so much easier not having sex for a while. You didn't have to think about it, worry about it, or add it to the list of chores that has grown with your beautiful new family. Sex was just another thing you could put off while you adjusted to your babyfied life. But now it's time to stop putting it off and start getting off.

If you're a woman you may be feeling much like Heidi did after the birth of her first daughter; sleepless and sexless, over-whelmed and overused. The physical and emotional demands of childbirth, motherhood, and nursing often conspire to be the anti-sexy. You're freaked out about your body, your plumbing, and your moods; and you're so tired you can barely see straight. And while some of you might be curious about starting things up again, or long to be close with your partners again, for others sex is the furthest thing from your mind. Except, of course, when your partner brings it up. Again. And again.

> **Sex, sex, sex. My husband has a one-track mind. Sometimes I'm so fed up, I feel like I'm ready to pull a Lorena Bobbitt and be done with the whole thing for once and all. But then I just smile and kiss him and tell him he's putting me in the mood in for a second child and that does the trick just as well. In a matter of seconds he's off watching a rerun of *Two and a Half Men*.**
>
> **EMILY, 35**

If you're a guy you might be feeling, well, hard up, horny, and ready to get back in there. Sort of. You've been through your own changes. Many of you have been subsisting on a junk diet of power bars and porn during the last six weeks—you've been taking matters into your own hands quite literally, and you're kind of used to fast-forwarding to the money shot and getting yourself off in less than sixty seconds. Compared to the rest of your new, baby-crazed life, those sixty seconds are like your own little spa day complete with happy ending. Will you be able to say the same about sex with the mother of your child? Even just that phrase—"mother of your child"—takes a little getting used to. It can definitely add to your anxiety about the sex to come: Are you going to get a mouthful of warm breast milk? How is everything holding up down there?

> It was a war zone in the delivery room. I was in awe of my wife, but I admit I was also pretty freaked out. It took a while to see her in the same light again.
>
> STEVE, 34

The physical and mental changes couples go through after having or adopting a baby can rock even the sexiest of constitutions, leaving a wake of confusion for both parties. With so much going on it might be easier to think that if you just put sex on hold for another couple months, if you just wait a little longer, then things will get back to what they were before. (It won't, trust us!) We're here to say, now is the time, now is the place, now is the beginning of something very different but equally sweet and often even more so. This is an opportunity to start fresh, to build a new foundation for sexual fun, based on the closeness, honesty, and patience you're gaining. (You are gaining it, trust us.) Getting back in the saddle is daunting—and you're right to expect a little chafing. But with a little finesse, a lot of love, some tack, and plenty of tact, you'll be barreling around again in no time.

BACK IN THE SADDLE: WHAT MOMS WANT DADS TO KNOW
We Might Want Another Six Weeks

I delivered my baby naturally—when the Doc gave me the green light to have sex again my body was like, errrrr, red light!

AMY, 29

I was floored at the lack of sex drive after my second child was born. I remember watching a sex scene on TV and really truly being baffled by the act.

SERENA, 37

Okay, you guys want sex . . . so we've heard. Your little hints are getting more and more obvious. And while some of us might be ready or curious about getting back in there, many others of us are just trying to survive the days! I remember wishing I had another six weeks of not dealing, a "get out of jail free" card I could hand to JB to avoid dealing with sex altogether. As I said in the introduction, how could I tell him about all my concerns and hang-ups about getting sexual again when I barely knew what was going on with me myself? Adding to any stress we may be feeling about "getting back in there" is the idea that we are somehow letting you down. Believe us, you don't have to point out we haven't had sex— we're most likely very well aware of that—and we're just trying to figure out what's going on with our old sexy selves. We're also trying to figure out how to adjust to our new roles, and our new bodies, how to function on no sleep and generally navigate a gazillion other things that take our minds and bodies a million miles from sex. The truth is, many of us *want* to want sex . . . we just . . . don't. And if that's hard for you, it's downright confounding to us. We worry that because we don't want sex maybe something is wrong with us. We wonder if our desire will ever return, and worry about what will happen if it doesn't. Will you lose interest? How long will you put up with this drought before you drift off into cyberspace or meet a sexy young mom at the playground? Will we end up in some nunnery? Our imaginations get the better of us and we think everyone else is having mind-blowing, chandelier-hanging sex.

Heads up, guys: It's a bummer to not feel like the sex goddesses we once were. We want to be right there with you, to make you happy and connect and get back to those rockin' times . . . but often it just ain't happening. Contrary to what you might think, if we've lost our libidos it probably actually has very little to do with you. It's not because you're not attractive,

or that we're trying to drive you crazy. This new not-wanting-or
-even-thinking-about-sex thing is pretty weird for many of us
too, and honestly, a little old-fashioned release would probably
do us well at this stressed-out point. But once again, it just ain't
happening.

> I have a hard time portraying to my husband exactly why I
> am just not interested, basically ever. Not because I don't
> think he is adorable; he's a hottie! Not because he is doing
> anything (specific) wrong.
>
> TERESA, 40

> Is it me? Should I change my deodorant? Should I go get
> some of that hair dye for men and get rid of the gray? Sure,
> my wife keeps saying, it's not you, it's me, but I can't help but
> feeling I just don't get her wheels spinning anymore
>
> CHRIS, 42

We're Nervous Ninnies

> I had scarring from tearing during the birth. It really hurt
> every time we made love. I thought, okay, my sex life is over.
>
> JENNA, 34

> I pushed out an eleven-pound baby! I'm so stretched out I
> don't feel anything anymore.
>
> MONICA, 27

I had a C-section and the scar took so long to heal. Even
after it was "healed" it was still sore whenever my husband
brushed against it.

ALEXA, 36

Even if we've gotten to the place where we can wrap our heads
around having a good time in bed, some of us worry that our
bodies might not cooperate once we're actually there. We've
felt that hard thing poking us in the back. What is sex going
to feel like? Will it even work? What's going on with our
plumbing down there? We've been stretched, cut, pulled,
pushed; will we feel anything? Will we feel too much? Will it
hurt?

Case in point: I hit that famous six-week mark (with my
second child) just as I was writing this. So how did things
play out? I have to admit I was worried. After all, I'm supposed to be The Naughty Mommy . . . would my strategies
hold up? While I'm certainly not a crazy sexy woman these
days, I know I'm more game than I was at this same point
last time. The thing I was most worried about in terms of
getting back in the game was that it would be physically uncomfortable—making me not want to do it again! To keep
things cool I told JB to get inside me, but not to expect anything from it—I just wanted to see how it felt. He was game,
so we lay there naked with him inside me being very practical and scientific about it. While it wasn't passion unleashed,
there was something about being that close and laughing
with him about it that actually made it work. As it turns out,

it was uncomfortable to have him inside me—I was very dry and it had been a while— but by easing into it and keeping things light we had a good time. I didn't see stars or anything, but as far as first time back into things go, I'd give it a decent thumbs up.

No Cover = No Lover

Speaking of nerves: There is nothing like the prospect of getting ourselves knocked up again to put fear in the libidos of even the bravest women. Therefore, here's your new motto, guys: No Cover = No Lover. In case you were wondering (and you should be), a woman can get pregnant again as early as two or three weeks after delivery, even if her period hasn't resumed. This is not something we want to happen. Our job is to carry and birth the darn things, your job right now is to keep it from happening again! Breast-feeding will naturally decrease your chances of getting pregnant, but it certainly won't eliminate the possibility. Also known as lactational amenorrhea, this technique is most effective when breast-feeding is the only source of nutrition (no formula), and when the breast is the main source of pacification. Even then we've all heard stories of how those "Irish twins" in the family came to be. If you are not breast-feeding, you can generally start taking birth control pills when you get your period again. If you are breast-feeding, you'll want to talk to a health care provider about the best time to resume, but right now your best bet will be a condom and some good old-fashioned cover for going under covers.

We Are Tired; Really, Really, Really Tired

Here's the sad truth: Many of us moms would rather sleep than "sleep with" you. Sleep deprivation has been used as torture, and why would we want to have sex after six weeks of being tortured each night? The overwhelming exhaustion of not sleeping and the constant demands of baby can make us feisty and say things like: You want sex? We want nap. And more nap. And more nap. Then maybe sex. And while statements like these are sure to engender frustrated responses from equally exhausted partners, what we're really trying to say is: This is really hard. I need help. Please don't put any more demands on me because I can barely keep my head above water as it is and I really don't want to let you down. The reality is, baby boot camp has most likely worn both of us out. We're deep in battle fatigue. Baby exhaustion can make us prickly about these issues, and can make both of us miss the invisible contributions we both make to keep things running smoothly.

We Don't Feel Like a Nat-ur-al Woman

Unless you're talking hairy caveman natural, which is probably not what Aretha Franklin meant. It's hard for us to wrap our heads around the idea that you really want us. On any given day many of us feel like, hey, I wouldn't want me, why would anyone else? Chances are we haven't showered or brushed our teeth, our bodies have bounced around, not back, and in general we feel less yummy and more yucky. Things like trouble with "dispatching our cargo" can leave us feeling bloated and yucky, not to mention making intercourse a little uncomfortable. Sometimes we don't feel as "fresh" as we'd like. It's time to give us plenty of shower time before you come in and join us, it's time to be patient while we figure out how to use these new bodies of ours. And for heaven's sake, if a woman gently redirects you when you try to kiss her somewhere, don't push it or demand to know. We have our reasons. There's nothing like having to say, "Actually, honey, I don't want you to grab my ass because my hemorrhoids are acting up and that's just too close for comfort" to ruin an otherwise sexually fun exploration.

Practice Breast Practices

Love is a battlefield, man! And often a battle over . . . breasts! What a joy it was when the titty fairy first came in pregnancy; all those boobs aplenty . . . until the irony hit that they were off limits. Sorry, guys! While breast-feeding can be a real bummer for dads and add to feelings of being left out or having to temporarily share something that was once yours exclusively, the key word there is *temporarily*. As in most of parenting this is where the mantra, "this too shall pass," should be muttered daily. Before long, you and your girl's girls will be Breast Friends Forever again.

Now is the time to focus on other parts of the body you find hot. And while you might be missing out, your child is getting exactly what she or he needs. Here are just a few of the benefits:

- Breast-fed babies have fewer colds and ear infections (which means fewer nights up with crying baby, which means more nights up with you . . .)
- The nutrients in breast milk help build the baby's brain and immune system (see first statement)
- Breast milk is always the right temperature and ready to serve (you don't have to waste time sterilizing bottles or running to the store for formula, which leaves more time for . . . ?)

Breast-feeding is also good for Mom:

- Reduces her risk of breast, uterine, and ovarian cancer
- Burns calories (300–500 per day!)
- Helps with bonding (*bonding*, guys, not bondage!)
- Saves money (which means more to spend on libido boosters like massages, meals out, and house cleaners . . .)

BACK IN THE SADDLE: WHAT DADS WANT MOMS TO KNOW

We Want Sex (Obviously)

As a sex therapist I've worked with loads of guys who have cheated on their wives, many during the months following the birth of a child. And while cheating is bad enough, doing so with a new baby at home seems particularly vile and selfish—punishable by chemical castration. Which is why so many new dads come to see me wracked with guilt, as if I were a priest in the confessional. And while I can't provide absolution or forgiveness, I can listen. So what do these "ninth circle of hell" cheaters have to say? That they weren't looking for sex as much as they were looking for an emotional connection. For many guys, though certainly not all, his cheating heart really is all about his heart.

So yes, we want sex. But not for the obvious reasons. We're really not that interested in sex for the sake of sex. At least not just that. If all that mattered was getting off, we'd probably just stick with our hassle-free sixty-second spa day and get "graphic with our graphics." Contrary to popular belief, men don't need sex just because they need to stick their thing in something else every so often. Men need sex for the same reasons women need men to really listen: To prove that they're not alone, to share an intimate moment, to be noticed and seen as real human beings under all this parent mess. It's feedback for us, and when that loop gets cut off, we tend to get all loopy. As a culture, we're always talking about how much easier it is for guys to separate love and sex, but very often the opposite is true: Love and sex are not divisible, but inextricably bound together. Making love and feeling love are one and the same. Sex takes us to a place where words cannot follow and is the only authentic expression of romantic love we really know. For guys, sex is language all of its own, and if prior to kids we had grown accustomed to conversing in, say, extemporaneous verse, suddenly we're forced to operate within the confines of a haiku.

We Want to Cuddle and Reconnect . . . Really

Okay, ladies, I know it's hard to take this one seriously. Even Lisa, my wife, doesn't believe it. In fact, when she read this point in the original manuscript, she wrote in the margin, "You are a liar! You don't cuddle! Ha ha!" Lisa repeatedly told me that my idea of cuddling lasts all of five seconds before I make a move for her crotch. Lately when we're in bed (and there doesn't happen to be a five-year-old between us) and I ask her to come roll over my way for a few minutes—"I just want to hold you"—I might as well be "the boy who cried cuddle." And maybe I do try to go for more, but that doesn't mean I don't care about the cuddle.

Guys who were never big on cuddling in the first place (except of course in the early days when they were trying to get down your pants) are as surprised as anyone to discover that now that there is someone else competing for your time and attention (never mind they're only two feet tall), they yearn for the emotional connection that comes along with the physical intimacy of a simple snuggle. Sure, all things considered, we'd prefer to have sex and then cuddle. And for some men, admittedly, the cuddle is welcome because it gives us hope that there's a glimmer of possibility that sex could follow . . . but we'll take the cuddle when there isn't time for more; in fact, we need the cuddle to keep us tuned in, turned on, connected, and on course. Regular touching makes us feel wanted. We know you're on overload with the physical demands of being a mom, but just a little affection goes a long way toward making us feel like we still matter as much as our small and lovable competition.

And cuddling doesn't have to happen in bed. A snuggle on the couch or a nice, long, unexpected hug (and kiss) while we're doing the dishes can be just as good for making us feel connected. So can a playful slap on the behind or grabbing another favorite part. Bringing some touch back helps bring the love back, and we men need this. We know it can feel like the last thing in the world you want to do, but too often, being a dad feels like one long constant interruption—especially when it's the end of the night and we've finally made it to bed, only to have baby monitors beeping in the dark, scary monsters sending our kids into our beds, and desert-parched voices desperately calling out for a glass of water. Even when we're asleep, it seems as if there's always something getting between us and you and it doesn't take much for a "cuddle crack" in our relationship to become a serious gap. So come on: Give us a cuddle. And don't worry if it leads to an erection poking you in the back. We may talk a big game, but at the end of the day we're often just as tired as you are.

Without frequent touch—for example, when mates are apart—the brain's dopamine and oxytocin circuits and receptors can feel starved. Couples may not realize how much they depend on each other's physical presence until they are separated for a while.... In both males and females, oxytocin causes relaxation, fearlessness, bonding, and contentment with each other. And to maintain its effect long-term, the

brain's attachment system needs repeated, almost daily acti-
vation through oxytocin stimulated by closeness and touch....
Activities such as caressing, kissing, gazing, hugging, and
orgasm can replenish the chemical bond of love and trust.
LOUANN BRIZENDINE, M.D., *THE FEMALE BRAIN*

We're Nervous Too

Many of us guys worry about, er, mechanical malfunctions.
It's been a while—what if our tire gets a flat, or we find ourselves suddenly doing a Lance Armstrong across the finish
line? What if we start, then things go sour and we're left feeling a little . . . blue? What if we hurt you, or you feel different?
It doesn't help that we've been checking out that porn and
watching Captain Long-Dong go at it. How can we compete
with that? In short, we still have the same complexes we've
always had, maybe even more so. We wonder if you've ever
faked it, if we're too small, if we make you happy. It might not
be something we're ready to shout about, but the truth is,
we're feeling a little sensitive too. And sometimes just the anticipation of a poor performance is all it takes for it to become a self-fulfilling prophecy. Sex therapists call this
"spectatoring"—when someone watches their own engagement in the sexual event, rather than being in the moment
itself. And yes, sports fans, it also usually comes with typical
spectator behavior, such as criticizing, judging, evaluating,
and, of course, heckling. You've been out of the game for six
weeks, or more—it's only natural you're nervous about the
upcoming season.

We Want It to Be Sexy

After my son was born, I realized that what I missed most wasn't the bonking, but the whole lovemaking part. Not only do I have a new appreciation for all the aspects of foreplay I used to ignore, but I've also become more of a romantic than my wife.

NOAH, 32

It's cheesy, yes. And admittedly many men are not natural born romantics. But really, this is sort of a special moment. It's been a while. First, for many of us, there was all that scheduled, fertility-based "conceiving sex." Then came some good, some fantastic, some totally awkward "pregnancy sex," and now we have the baby to contend with. When we finally get a chance to be intimate again, we want it to be sexy and special. Some of us would rather have no sex than more half-assed sex. So let's make sex sexy again. We want to see you as sexy mama again, not just as Mommy.

Some Things We Used to Love Doing to You Just Seem, Well, Sort of, Kind of, Icky

Okay, even though some people call me Mr. She Comes First, let's just say it—we're not sure about the whole oral sex thing. Brave cunnilinguists we may be, but last we saw, things were pretty hectic down there. Not to mention the pregnancy, when there were those shifts in taste and smell. Hey, not to say that the last point about your sexiness isn't true, but let's just see where things go.

That said, on a good note, if we do happen to end up in Cupid's cave, relax. Don't worry about us—while you might be self-conscious about certain changes down there, once we're in the moment, a neurochemical cocktail of arousal takes over and you'll more than likely find us really happy to be there. The truth is, most guys love the feeling of closeness that's part of oral sex. And especially if we're worried about mechanical malfunction, calling in for oral backup may be just the thing we need. But know we may need to dip a toe (or rather tongue) in those waters before we're ready to dive in. My personal philosophy can be summed up in three words: Viva la Vulva, and that's true even when said vulva has gone through some natural variation.

> I've always loved going down on my wife and she's always really dug it too, and I really didn't have any hesitation doing it after the birth of our daughter, but funny enough it was my wife who was nervous and skittish about it. I had to give her a lot of reassurance that I really wanted to go down on her and that everything was fine down there.
>
> RON, 35

SEX RX FOR THE LADIES: FLEX YOUR MUSCLES FRENCH-STYLE

Voulez-vous couchez avec moi?

"LADY MARMALADE"

It's common practice in France to check a woman's pubo-coccygeus (PC) muscles as part of a regular checkup after childbirth. Here, too, often we don't hear anything about getting things back in shape besides "Kegels, Kegels, Kegels!" Did you know there are physical therapists who specialize in pelvic floor issues? Fight for your right for good sex! And for more comprehensive health care! Can you say, "Ooh la la"?

PS, or Shall we Say PC . . . To work out your PC muscles closer to home, check out the DVD "Sweet Moves," a sexercise video specifically geared toward strengthening and toning the muscles used during sex! This video is outtasite, man! The workout combines a vigorous workout with glitter, glam, great music, humor, and sex-positive philosophy. It's rated R, and definitely adult, but it's not porn. Also check your local sex store catalog—there are some great PC muscle builders now, like sexpert Betty Dodson's Vaginal Barbell. These can be multipurpose, doubling as sex toys. And you know how we like to multitask! Also, Betty's book *Sex for One* is still the definitive classic on female masturbation. So if pleasuring yourself has never been your thing, or you just need some specific exercises to help you get relaxed and back in the self-groping groove, pick up a copy and give your fingers a walking tour of your vulva.

FOR THE GUYS: SLOW RIDE . . . TAKE IT EASY . . .

It took nine months to make a baby; it's going to take more than a single night to remake your sex life. It's time to slow down. Let her ease back into touch by giving her a non-sexual massage. (NON-SEXUAL, GUYS. NO WANTON GROPING!) If she gets turned on, great, but don't expect to have things go further than that. A big takeaway here for you guys is to take things slowly—ease in; literally, not just metaphorically. Not only might the sex be a little (or a lot) painful for her, but the anxiety around that potential pain might be even higher.

Also, guys, you should know that if the first time is painful, it makes it all the harder to jump back in the next time around. Painful intercourse is one main cause of sexual anxiety in women and a huge libido dampener. So it's in both your interests to keep things nice and gentle. And remember, sex doesn't have to include intercourse. This is a good time for some partner DIY or enjoying a little five-finger shuffle. Use your limitations as opportunities to explore new paths to pleasure. With a new sex life also comes a need for a little more sexual boldness—a willingness to go where you haven't gone before. Making sex sexy again is a process, but it also happens naturally once we get the ball rolling.

TIP: Because of low estrogen levels, nursing can make a woman feel dry, even if she's excited, so if you haven't been lubricating your sex life in the past, now's the time to start.

SEX RX TO DO TOGETHER: BABES IN TOYLAND . . .

Or Toys in Babeland, one of our favorite sex toy stores. Your mission: Find the best lubricant for you. This is a playful thing you can do together without actually having to have sex! Of course you could also just go to your local drug store and buy diapers and lubricant, or shop online, but we think a sex toy shop will be a lot more fun and inspiring. Regardless of where you're doing your lube buying, employ a little consumer awareness as there are lots of different lubricants available on the market:

- Petroleum-based lubes such as Vaseline. These are quite common, but can also irritate the vulva and degrade latex-based condoms. So not the best choice for gloved love, which should be a must.
- Water-based lubricants with glycerin, which provides for a slightly sweet taste. Anytime a lube is flavored or uses a warming agent, you can be sure glycerin (either in the form of a natural oil or a synthetic) is being used. But glycerins, especially synthetic, can also trigger a yeast infection. And do you really need to be worrying that right now?

- Plain and simple water-based lubricants. Probably the safest choice, except they dry out quickly, so you need to have a lot on hand. Best water-based lubricant: saliva.
- Silicone-based lubricants last the longest, are safe to use with condoms, and a little goes a long way. But they also generally include some scary-sounding ingredients: Cyclpentasiloxane, Dimethicone, Dimethiconaol. And while it's true that silicone lubrication does not penetrate the skin, if you're a new mom and breast-feeding, we say stay away. We pride ourselves on being scientific, but also a wee bit superstitious.

For years, I couldn't get my boyfriend to walk into a sex toy shop with me. Whenever I asked, he'd just smile and say, "Mission impossible." But since having a baby and being in an on-and-off sex rut for more than a year, when I suggested we stock up on some lube and other fun stuff, he grabbed my hand and said let's go. It took a baby to make his mission impossible a mission possible.

KATI, 29

I never knew shopping could be so fun.

GARY, 33

IN CONCLUSION

Many people call the three months after the birth of a baby the "fourth trimester"—a time of continued growth and change that for many of us leads to the start of a slump that begins to take off on its own. As a couple, it's time to grab the reins and get this bad boy under control. Understanding where your partner is coming from physically and mentally, being patient with each other (and yourselves!), and keeping lines of communication open about where you are sexually can help steer those changes away from "no sex" to "mo' sex"—or at least "mo' better" sex. And before you know it you'll be back to the ol' yippe-ki-yi-yay and ready to play.

DIAGNOSE THIS!
STATE OF YOUR UNION

You know the phrase "use it or lose it," but how can you lose something that, for many of us, wasn't ever there in the first place? To get where you're going you have to first know where you are. Take this quiz and find out how your union is really doing.

As a couple, try to remember those days way back, before kids, before hormone-crazy pregnancy. What was your sex life really like? There are no right or wrong answers, no cheat sheet. The point of this quiz is to start a conversation. You just might be surprised by each others' selective memories.

BEFORE THE BABY:

1. You emailed, called, or texted each other . . .
   A. just because
   B. evenings and weekends
   C. hardly ever—why waste precious minutes?

2. If sex was a package, you would have sent it . . .
   A. priority mail!
   B. regular two-day
   C. ground—who cares when it gets there

3. If you flew like you fucked, you'd be flying . . .
   A. first class—mile-high club, baby!
   B. business—kinda perky
   C. coach—limited legroom. Need we say more?

4. Talking about sexual needs, wants, and whatnots for you was . . .
   A. easy as pie
   B. bittersweet
   C. ice cream headache!

5. A typical anniversary celebration included . . .
   A. staying up late talking and talking, wink, wink

B. renting *Look Who's Talking* and snuggling

C. talking about the bills

6. When it came to showing affection, you were like:

   A. love birds

   B. gorillas—picky and patty

   C. fish, belly up

MOSTLY ANSWER A:

The good news is you've got game. The bad news is the baby is forcing an extremely long time out. More good news: With a little help and insight you'll be getting it on again.

MOSTLY ANSWER B:

Okay. You used to like each other just fine. That's good. But it's not great. The good news? You can take the stuff you learn here back to your relationship to not only blow past the baby hump, but to shoot into an even more passionate and satisfying place.

MOSTLY ANSWER C:

Well, you've got some work to do—but we expect that. The good news is, you're reading this book. The bad news is, getting back to where you were isn't enough. You've got to see this challenge as an opportunity to fix what was lackluster before. It's time to break out the polish and get rubbin'. With a little elbow grease, and perhaps some other lubrication products, your love life will be shining even brighter than before.

CHAPTER TWO

Psych 911: Why New Parenthood Can Be a Crash Course in the Blues

LIGHTS, CAMERA ... ACTION?

Picture this: New lovers laugh and giggle in bed together, a tangled mess of body parts and warmth. It's a classic romantic scene—if not quite *The Way We Were* then certainly *The Way We Are*. Even without speaking, the pair communicate as one, subsumed in the rapture of new love. That is, until Dad attempts to get into bed with them. In a battle for territory with his nubile foe, Dad tries to garner a kiss (or more) of his own. The resolution is swift and decisive: The intruder is vanquished, the hairless wonder wins again. Without achieving even a lick, the lowly third wheel hands victory over to the tiny lover and retreats to his den to lick his wounds—and maybe watch a little Internet porn.

HEIDI: *I remember wanting to make out with my baby more than my husband in those early months. She was so delicious, and he smelled like salami. She cooed, he snored. He was of the outside world—but she WAS my world.*

IAN: *Tell me about it—both our kids end up in bed with us, and every morning without fail, I'm woken to the sounds of a little smooch festival. It's a little threesome of kissing and cooing between Lisa, Owen, and Beckett. The upside? I'm the first to grab a shower.*

> **I'm not crazy; I was just a new mother adjusting to my new role of Mother Love.**
>
> SHARI, 31

It's easy to drift away from each other when you realize that your smooth two-person Harley of a relationship has turned into a slow tippy tricycle. More sexual speed bumps pop up as new roles and relationships are further established, making real connection that much harder. Navigating this new vehicle can sometimes feel like a mess of loose (cannon) washers and lost (sexy) screws. The truth is if it feels like something has come between you lately, it has! Something cute, but formidable nonetheless. Too often moms don't realize how it feels to be the left-out third wheel, or what it means to men when the intimacy they expect and need is directed to someone else. For many guys, that's when it's clear that sex starts meaning a lot more than just sex! And too often dads underestimate the huge psychological changes many mothers go through as they figure out how to survive and hopefully thrive in the new and all-encompassing role of "mother," not to mention the hormones.

I love my new baby girl, but I'm not in love with her. Is that bad for me to say? Should I feel guilty? I'm not saying I wouldn't step in front of a bus for her, but as deep as my love goes, I just don't feel that *Romeo and Juliet* all-encompassing sense of infatuation. My wife? Now that's another story. She's definitely feeling it at Shakespearean levels.

SETH, 37

Beyond navigating the blues and all its many shades, new parenthood has ample opportunity for emotional button pressing—it makes us take a hard look at the baggage and sloppy gear we're carrying; the things from our own childhoods that may be holding us up or weighing us down. As challenging as it can be to face all these issues, there is a lot of room here to bust some wheelies and grow a little, or a lot, on your own and together. There's room to break out of the sidecar role with each other, to maintain your special grown-up bond and your place in each other's hearts—without leaving too much killer road rash.

PSYCH 911: WHAT MOMS WANT DADS TO KNOW
It's All About the Baby

After giving birth to my daughter Ramona, every part of my body seemed to scream: Take care of this baby . . . don't make another one! It's biology in action, folks! It's the reason we moms say things like: "I could just eat you up"—we practically could. Babies taste delicious to us. They smell delicious to us. Our breasts, our hormones, our minds are devoted to baby. Our bodies mold to match theirs. This is why cheap tricks, like turning the monitor down, won't win us over or work. We have internal monitors based on species survival that compel us to check on the baby. This is a beautiful and necessary part of the attachment process. And while it's great for the mommy-baby bonding that's happening, it can be pretty brutal on the mommy-daddy bonding that is not happening.

> Baby this, baby that, blah, blah, baby—was my wife ever able to use a sentence before this baby came along? Is there no other noun than "baby" in her entire vocabulary?
>
> JONAS, 33

You can call it motherotica. Or don't if that's too weird. But without being creepy, it's important to acknowledge this erotic bond between Mom and baby. This is not to be confused with the "erotic dancer" kind of erotic, but rather an intimate energy that passes from one person to another. As Freud defined it, *eros* is a life force that motivates us to create and to love, and for many mothers, the energy that goes into doting on, dressing, feeding, cooing at, and coddling a baby is a powerful expression of eros. There was a time when we wouldn't let you guys out wearing that tie. Now we're so caught up in dressing our little one, we may not even notice that Dad has gone a full week without showering. It's important to note that a good part of this re-direction of erotic energy is thanks to those pesky hormones again. During breast-feeding, oxytocin levels go through the roof. Oxytocin, also known as the "cuddle hormone," serves a variety of different purposes at different times: to stimulate a deep sense of emotional connection between lovers during sex (oxytocin levels are very high throughout arousal and particularly during orgasm), to provoke the uterine contractions of childbirth (why many ob-gyns often recommend orgasms to induce labor), and most important, to stimulate the let-down reflex that enables a mom to feed her baby and bond intensely throughout the process. Even if a woman has not given birth or is not breast-feeding, just cuddling her baby will do the same thing.

So what's a dad to do? The key is to work with nature here, guys, not against it! Appeal to our baby obsession by stepping up the superdad drill. I've heard women say, "My husband looks so sexy when he's playing with the baby." Rather than withdrawal, woo us by engaging with the baby. Lie next to us and coo along instead of cawing about feeling left out. As we tell the tots, don't be a whine-ocerus. This is where we're at right now. Lie there with us now and we're more likely to lie with you when the opportunity arises.

We Are Not Really the Boss of Everything

Due to something called the "snowball effect" and good old-fashioned roles and gender expectations, often moms become the defacto expert on all things baby. The truth is that we don't know that much more about the baby than you do . . .

we just do it more often, so we look like the expert. And soon, it's easier for us to just do something than have to watch you suffer through figuring out what works. (Many of us figured it out in the privacy of our mistakes.) It's hard for us to step back and let you work things out with the baby. Our mama bear instincts make us want to take over, to never have to hear them cry, to scold you every time you do something "wrong" with the baby. Here's a secret: Often we're just plain insecure so we're overcompensating, faking it, needing to be right and in control since so much of mothering feels out of control. We need your support ("You're doing great," "Wow, you really know how to get her to sleep," etc.), but we also need you to step up and challenge the status quo.

Don't go for that whole selective incompetence thing! Yes, it's easy to walk away with a hangdog feeling, but chances are it will be better for us all if you say, clearly: "I need to know how to do this too" or "No, let me try it." Some of us may even have to physically leave the room (or even the house!) because we're so overinvolved and into micromanaging your relationship with the baby. This overinvolvement is not healthy, for you, the baby, or us. Don't let us do it. If you tread just right, stepping up will not only help our family, but actually make you look super studly to us. And that's a good thing.

> **Okay, admittedly, I'm a Taurus, but why does my wife have to make me feel like a bull in a china shop every time I hold my own child?**
>
> EVAN, 26

My husband read every baby book—he was suddenly the expert and I had to hear what I was doing wrong with the baby all the time.

SARAH, 25

We Really Don't Want to Cuddle, Naked or Not

Despite touching everyone else all day, I can't remember the last time I touched myself.

KERRY, 30

When my kids were little I spent most of my days in intimacy overload!

GENINE, 41

Okay, we know there's nothing quite like someone saying "please don't touch me" in response to an affectionate hug to really turn the room cold. But if we have young children, then chances are that most of the day we've been poked, prodded, pooped on, sucked on, and had the energy sucked out of us. We don't even want to pet the dog, much less you. We are "touched out" by the physical demands of parenting and the little milk vampire that depends on us. But it's not only that; many of us are actually "intimacied" out. We get so much intense interaction and touch from the baby that we need it from you about as much as a log. That, while sweet for the mama-baby bond, obviously can really get in the way of making sweet love. Remember, though: It's not personal. It's just that sometimes we're all filled up from other sources. (That's why it's best to hit on us when we've had some space, when we've been away from the baby. . . .)

> Last night, I tried to hug my girlfriend for the first time in like two weeks—she immediately recoiled and said she was fed up always being touched. Well, EX-CUUUUSE me for even trying!!
>
> JACK, 29

We Don't Like Always Being Debbie Downer

> I don't miss the sex but feel sad about disappointing him in this way.
>
> CAITLIN, 36

So we hear that it sucks to be the one who initiates sex all the time. But it also really sucks being the one to say no all the time. It puts all the pressure, and really, all the control in our hands. And our hands are full already! You might feel yourself "spectatoring" but we too often feel the specter of "when's the last time we had sex?" breathing down our necks. Here's something to consider: How do you initiate? Are you initiating to really get the connection going or to be in the right? Or maybe to remind us that it's been two weeks, three days, and forty-seven minutes since we last had sex? This is a time for finesse and feelings, not statistics. Saying, "We never have sex anymore," can put a woman in defense mode—it can make it appear that having sex with us is a birthright of yours, not something fun we do together. Hearing our loved one say, "Boy, do I miss you. You are still so sexy," gets the juices flowing a lot more. One makes it seem like sex is what you want. Another makes it seem like we're the one you want.

In the case of JB and me, after burning out on always being the one to initiate sex (and the fights that followed), JB decided he would take matters into his own hands (literally!) and go on a "sex initiation strike." At first I scoffed, doubting he would stick it out for more than a day. After a week, I warned him that, left up to me, sex just might never happen again. But after week three something really strange happened: I wanted him to come on to me! I missed his advances. I started flirting with him, cuddling more, pressing up against previously "dangerous" body parts. Not *having* to say no all the time actually made space for me to think about saying yes. When I finally broke and attacked him, I was surprised by how nice it was and how much I took his invitations for granted. While a sex strike might be a little extreme for some (and end up nowhere for others) I think there's something to be said for giving a girl a little room to find her own way back to the bedroom.

I Need a Playdate—With Myself

Children are indeed a source of nurturance for adults. Their unconditional love infuses our lives with a heightened sense of meaning. The problem arises when we turn to them for what we no longer get from each other: a sense that we're special, that we matter, that we're not alone. When we transfer these adult emotional needs onto our children, we are placing too big a burden on them.

ESTHER PEREL, *MATING IN CAPTIVITY*

How do we, as mamas, justify our own needs and wants when our babies are so needy and wanty? How can we ease our minds around the fact that we want and need too?

LORI, 39

For some of us, mother-love is as good as a drug. It hits us in a place that leaves us feeling so right, it fill holes we had, it makes us complete. We can be so caught up in our role as mother that we forget there is any other side of us. Because it feels so right to be one with our little buddies, we forget we're actually separate. The lines have blurred, we are Mother with a capital *M* and nothing else seems to matter.

For others of us, though, this whole mother gig isn't what we thought it would be. We might have the baby blues, or just be exhausted or really just wish we were back at work where we know what we're doing. Or maybe we are back at work, and freaking out because we feel guilty or no longer the go-to parent. Maybe the supermom act is starting to crack, with work and baby taking up everything we have to give. When we do find time where we're not being climbed on/sucked/poked/jabbered at, too often we immediately dive into the ol' to-do's rather than just taking a moment for ourselves. Whatever department your partner falls into, helping her to remember she is someone other than mother is helpful and necessary for our sanity and libidos.

Did Somebody Say Blues . . . ?

In essence, I feel pretty useless. My mothering abilities are arguable, my patience level is zero, I have nothing interesting to say to anyone, and I hate looking in the mirror.

JOAN, 33

Postpartum depression (PPD) affects nearly 20 percent of women, so guys, help us keep an eye out for the signs. Most women let it go untreated. The rut we're in may have to do with a lot more than just sex, so use the sex rut as a starting point for looking for other symptoms:

- Does depression run in her family?
- Is she having problems sleeping, even though she's exhausted?
- Is she crying a lot, and not able to explain why or what's going on?
- Does she talk a lot about feeling judged as a mom, either by parents, family, or peers?
- Is she avoiding going out with the baby and generally isolating herself?
- Do you feel like she's trying to put on a "happy front"?

Not only is it important to support the mom who may be experiencing PPD (it often lasts up to six months), but it's also important to think about how to get her professional help—she may be a candidate for transdermal estrogen therapy, and certainly for psychological care. When we hear about PPD, it's often the extreme cases. But many women also suffer from just feeling down while we try to adjust to our new lives and roles. Lack of sleep, feeling overwhelmed or judged—or loss of identity, job, or body for that matter—can take their toll and add that crappy feeling. And feeling crappy is really bad for sex.

There are things you can do to help us feel better: Remind us to nap when the baby does. Help us out more around the house and with the baby. Encourage us to make friends with other moms or join a support group. This kind of "baby blues" usually goes away on its own. But the more serious postpartum depression can happen anytime within the first year after childbirth and requires professional help. A woman may have symptoms such as sadness, lack of energy, trouble concentrating, anxiety, and feelings of guilt and worthlessness. The difference between postpartum depression and the baby blues is that postpartum depression often affects a woman's well-being and keeps her from functioning well for a longer time. When the baby blues won't go away, and they seem to be getting more and more intense, it's time to see a doctor. Counseling, support groups, and medicines can all help.

PSYCH 911: WHAT DADS WANT MOMS TO KNOW
I've Got the Third-Wheel Blues

Don't forget, ladies, we were there when it all began. We were as revved up about this whole baby-making process as much as you were, if not more, remember? We had something to do with it. (Didn't we? Okay, let's not go there. We'll just have to accept that our newest addition bears a striking resemblance to the good-looking UPS guy with the wavy blonde hair.) We were ready for fatherhood, and enjoyed every second of assembling all that baby furniture, immersing ourselves in user manuals and carefully poring over the reviews of a million different gadgets and gizmos. We agonized over the attributes of a Maclaren versus a Bugaboo. Not only did we want to make way for the little prince or princess, we eagerly built the throne.

Sure, we heard all the stories about new parents being sleepless, sexless, hard up, and horny, but what we didn't fathom was the sheer sense of disconnection and disorientation that comes along with those things. Too often, this whole parenting thing can make a guy feel like an astronaut whose just had his lifeline cut—we're spinning off into space, alone and in the dark. And we're just not brought up to express our emotions or validate them in any way that can actually edge us toward the light at the end of the tunnel. Instead, we retreat a little further into darkness, operating out of an emotional deficit that makes it harder and harder to get out of the red, or in this case out of the blues. The lack of touch and physical intimacy, especially since you're all "touched out," just adds to our sense of being a third wheel. We often can't help but feel that we were merely rehearsal partners for the baby and you—an understudy for a role that was always intended for a bigger star. And regardless of our own love for this new romantic lead, it's a blow to get pushed out of the spotlight.

> After the baby I kept my libido and he lost his. He had fallen in love with a new babe.
>
> REBECCA, 40

> When I don't have sex or connect physically with my wife, I start to feel really alone in the world.
>
> JAMES, 28

Speaking of Feelings ... I've (Gulp) Got Some

As one of my patients, thirty-six-year-old Steve, observed:

> Before having a baby my wife used to dote on me to the point where it drove me nuts. I always joked about how I couldn't wait to have a baby with her so that she'd finally have someone other than me to shower with kisses and hugs. But when it happened, I felt totally cast aside and rejected (even though I couldn't admit it), and struggled with my own sense of immaturity at feeling this way. At first I thought it was all about sex, and not getting any, but

I soon realized it went deeper and had as much, if not more, to do with my past than the present. My wife comes from a big, loving family and a childhood home that was full of life and noise, but I was the latchkey kid of a single divorced mom who was distant and remote and always working to make ends meet. And even though I've always been much more prickly and standoffish about expressing my emotions, I think what ultimately attracted me to my wife was all the warmth and love that she had to give.

Many of us have made it this far without ending up in a therapist's office. The whole "first comes love, then comes marriage" part wasn't the problem. We had a lot of time to work out the relationship stuff and iron out the kinks along the way, and we'd like to think we got pretty good at it (relatively speaking) by the time you came along. That's not to say there isn't room for improvement, but after having some test-runs over a career of serially monogamous relationships, we got kind of used to being in our own skin and knowing our strengths and weaknesses when it came to love and sex. But now this whole "then comes the baby carriage" part of the equation has thrown us for a loop and we don't know what we know anymore. Being a new father creates a bleary-eyed state of déjà vu, one in which we're often remembering and reflecting upon our own childhoods, and brooding over the love we received, or too often didn't receive, way back when.

TIP: WATCH OUT FOR THE BIG MAN LIE

NOTHING'S WRONG. I'M FINE. We say this all the time. We sit on things. It's called self-silencing and bottling-up behavior, and it's classic third-wheel conversation— although we all know many of you women out there love this line as well. When you hear "nothing is wrong" or "I'm fine," it's a little moment when a damaged relationship could and should be repaired. This is really about knowing your feelings are valid, something men in particular struggle with. But if neither of you can turn to the other and really say what's bothering you, three months later you can find yourself in an affair. Too often the two phrases are conversation stoppers, and too often our partners are willing to let things rest there. But when you hear this line, your partner is more than likely looking for the attention he (or she) is pretending not to need.

Inside Every Man Is a Little Boy

While it makes us cringe to admit that we want to be mmm . . . mmmoth . . . mothered by you, there was a time when you doted on us in a way that was, well, mom-like. You helped us pick out new clothes, you inspired us to clean our rooms, you told us when we needed to shower, and you made us feel powerfully and unconditionally loved (even if we did come close to screwing it all up more than once). You brought out our inner child and let him play, but now it's time for him to go back inside his dark, dank little cave. The little one with the toothless smile seems to get his every need met, while ours go seemingly unnoticed. Why don't you just put the baby down for a minute and make some time for me, or at least stop worrying about the baby for a second? We need to know we still matter to you too. Just because we're fathers now doesn't mean we're able to give up being sons, or turning to you for a little mmm, mmm, mothering. (Gosh that's hard to say.)

And speaking of mothers . . .

Yours is the toppermost of the poppermost, but . . . I know you love your mother, (and so do I actually), but man it seems like since these little ones came along we're constantly playing catch-up with our respective clans. Just when we've been through our quarterly rotation of visits and catch-ups, the whole thing starts all over again. This is supposed to be *our* time. But too often it belongs to other people. Whenever "our time" is supposed to start, the phone rings, your friend drops by, a diaper needs to be changed . . . and you know we're already feeling like lowly third wheels much of the time. Let's be honest, having a baby is often an invitation to greater involvement from the in-laws. Having a child does mean you usually have to let family into your life in a bigger way—but you don't have to let them into the bedroom.

> I love my in-laws, but I hate the way my wife has to talk to her mother all the time, especially at night after the kids are finally asleep. That should be my time.
>
> JORDAN, 36

I'm Going to Throw a Real Fit Right Now
Because I Love You

Whether we consciously realize this, sometimes a good, old-fashioned fit is the only way to get your attention. For many of us, it's our attempt to fall back on the old reliable pattern of fighting and screwing, although in this case we're more liable to end up just fighting. Even without a baby a lot of women don't get why arguing often leaves so many guys all hot and bothered. But in the male brain, sexual arousal and aggression crisscross neural pathways, so arguing often triggers desire. The nerve tissue that transmits sexual stimuli is closely interlinked with the nerve tissue associated with aggression; so much so that it's difficult to tell the two apart. So sometimes arguing with you is just our way of approaching foreplay. Sometimes we don't really even want sex, we just want your attention, or more specifically we want to annoy you.

I guess having a baby brings out the baby in us. We know those constant nudges for sex get on your nerves, and frankly we're frequently trying to piss you off. If we can't get your positive attention, might as well get some negative attention. It beats nothing at all, which is pretty much what we've been settling for. Or think of it another way: It's not that we want to physically get off (although that would be nice too), but initiating sex is our way of letting you know we're still here. So show a little mercy. And if you're really kind, a little mercy sex.

Even before we had a baby and were both getting lots of sleep, my husband had a bad temper. Sex was his way of saying sorry, and I kind of liked it because it led to some of our most tender, intense connections. But now the arguing is out of control, and it's a constant commotion. I'm too tired to fight with him, and I'm definitely too tired to have sex. In terms of the big picture I get that he's crying out for attention, although he'd never admit it, but when you have a colicky baby crying all night, it kind of drowns out all other sounds.

ELIZABETH, 31

Don't Be Such a Gatekeeper

While it sounds like the name of a sci-fi movie, it is actually someone who unconsciously discourages his or her partner taking action in an attempt to retain control. Gatekeeping, also known as one-upping, is a common arguing strategy for parents, especially the one who spends more time doing the child care. Gatekeepers will often feel a need to show you how it's done, to point out the articles and books you should be reading, and use their expertise as a way of expressing anger and resentment. Also, in the face of a gatekeeper, a partner may end up being a self-silencer—bottling up emotions in an unhealthy manner, or simply giving up rather than feeling entitled to make a point. So very often you end up with a one-upper and a self-silencer. For the one-upper it's about being willing to hand over the keys and share the gatekeeping, and for the self-silencer it's about not holding things in and letting resentments brew to a boiling point. So give up the keys to the gate, and know that the Earth will continue to revolve around the Sun.

Initiating Sex All the Time Makes Me Feel Like Even More of a Third Wheel

We know that sex is not always on your radar. (Okay, that's an understatement.) So we end up lobbing a lot of sexual softballs in your direction knowing that most of them won't be in your sexual strike zone. But after a while, all that pitching starts to wear us down. We start to think maybe you really don't like us. Especially when you roll your eyes or sigh heavily when we even come near the topic of when we are going to have sex—or the way you recoil when we simply try to hug you. Stop treating us like we're some sort of sexual predator. Every now and then we'd love to know that you want it too—even a little. Because that means you love us too. As Cheap Trick might say—we want you to want us. . . . we'd love you to love us.

> **Pitching sex all the time wouldn't be so bad if the answer was always a resounding "You bet!"**
>
> MATT, 35

SEX RX FOR THE LADIES: INVENTORY CHECK

Who wants to give away a part of themselves when there's not much left to give? It's time to own up to ourselves and take a good look at our love/energy inventory. Are you nurturing your own sexuality and your relationship as well as your little ones? Here's an exercise to help you check in where you might be checking out.

As you go through your day, think about how you nurture and whether that energy goes to you, your partner, or your child. Now of course babies and kids need more, but this is a good way to see where the balance really lies. Take notes as you go along. At the end of the day, look at your list and see where you might be able to change. Once you've written through your day, flesh it out. Who gets most of your nurturing energy? Does it feel fair, knowing everyone's needs? Are there things that could be changed to move them to balance things out more? What do you think your partner's list would look like? For example, here's a classic Heidi day with nurturing notes:

- Snuggled and nursed the baby early in the morning (baby)
- Let husband sleep in rather than asking him to help with morning routine because he was up late working (husband)
- Stressful morning routine, making lunch and getting older child dressed (big girl)
- Starving! Ate a big lunch (self)
- Breast-fed forever, baby wouldn't nap (baby)
- Rushed to pick up big girl from school (big girl)
- Spent nap time on phone, called Mom back, cheered up depressed friend (others)

- Helped big girl with homework (big girl)
- Cooked dinner while kids screamed so we could all eat right at six when JB gets home (husband/kids)
- Took a bath (self)
- Put kids to bed, snuggles and kisses (kids)
- Watched lame TV, then bed (self—if you call that nurturing!)

Looking through my list, two things really struck me. First, I could do a better job of nurturing myself through the day. What I put down for self-nurturing really isn't that great; they're not big hitters for me to get me recharged. I'm definitely expending "nurture" energy inefficiently. Second, I noticed that although I put a couple spots down for nurturing JB, those aren't necessarily things he wants me to do—and worse, they take away from the self-nurturing! He agreed. When he looked at my list he said he wished he got more snuggles and kisses like the girls, and he would definitely trade sleeping in (which he never asked for), eating right at six (again, he never asked for this), and putting the girls to sleep (which I actually like doing) to make life less stressful for me, and more likely to give him more of the good stuff.

What does Ian's list look like? "Think about sex, then multiply times 1,000." Okay, and not just because a guy thinks about sex a thousand times a day. He's a sex therapist: He really does think about sex a thousand times a day. (But seriously, that's just a lame excuse to make up for the fact that he's a walking cliché, just like all the other millions of walking clichés out there.)

SEX RX FOR THE GUYS: FIGHT FOR YOUR RIGHTS, ER, ROOTS

As Ian said in the Introduction, the person initiating sex really is fighting for the relationship in some ways. But as Heidi said, there are better ways to go about it than whining. Start by writing a letter to your partner explaining what sex means to you. Don't be freaked out by the letter thing; you can just make a list and give her that. It's amazing what people who love you think is romantic. Use that. Write down the reasons you love sex with her and (exactly—don't be shy) what you look forward to as you get your groove back together. It might feel a little exposing, but the mind really is the biggest sex organ, and it sometimes takes a while for the body to follow. If you can't do the letter thing, find an honest moment to tell her what sex really means to you. The act of communicating this is like planting a little sexual seed. Now back off, give some time, and space, for things to take root.

SEX RX TO DO TOGETHER: ENOUGH IS (HOPEFULLY) ENOUGH

So how much sex is enough? How much sex are other people really having out there? While we know some of you would love statistics to round out your arguments for and against, the truth is there isn't a magic number. It's also hard to get a real answer because people fib. Lots of people, less brave than you folks reading this, would rather pretend everything's fine and great than face the truth of their numbers. The "right" amount of sex for people to have is the right amount for each of you. Some couples are happy having sex 2.5 times a week, some need it every day to be happy, and some can go a month without it.

The problem comes when one person wants it more than the other. So when it comes to how much sex, the answer is enough is enough. If one or the other of you is feeling like it's not enough, here's an easy way to get things rolling: Go for a twenty-second hug. Really, that's all it takes to raise oxytocin levels and bond two people to each other. Couples who touch more end up having sex more. For those of you women out there saying, "Cuddle, right . . ." start with a non-naked one. All it takes is a twenty-second hug to get the oxytocin flowing in women, but men need to be hugged three times as much as women to get to similar levels. So start hugging, and try for a good minute of embracing. The idea is to build up a bank account of small touch-deposits during the day—you may be surprised at your desire to make a larger withdrawal at night.

IN CONCLUSION

As parenthood often shows us, we've got baggage, even when we thought all the suitcases were neatly stored and put away. Think of sex as your relationship's personal pack n' play—a way to stay connected while you deal with the issues. Our roles as "mom" and "dad" can be overwhelming, in both good and bad ways. How is it that something so right in our lives can leave us feeling so disconnected to each other at times? Once, the Woman Who Is Now Mom was a self-actualized individual who had clear lines between "self" and "other," and actually liked to be touched! Once, in the not so distant past, it was the Man Who Is Now Dad who was the recipient of all the oxytocin-induced tenderness his wife had to give. Rather than complain or give up entirely, it's time for both of you to fight the good fight; sex is important, connection is key—for yourselves, each other, and the havoc-wreaking little Diva (or Div-o) you can no longer imagine life without.

REAL LIFE GROWN-UP SELF-HELP EXERCISE: GET SOME ORDER IN YOUR LIFE

Let's face it. There are connections between our past and present lives. (No, not like Shirley MacLaine's past lives, we mean like your childhood lives, the way you grew up.) This is true of our sex lives, too. In his book *Sex Recharge,* Ian came up with a process called reORDERing to help make some of these connections. We think the same process can help you when things start to get freaky (freaky bad, not freaky sexy). Check it out and reORDER your thoughts and actions when the going gets tough:

- <u>O</u>bserve both the situation at hand with your partner and how outside influences may have shaped your behaviors
- <u>R</u>ecognize recurring patterns and what triggers them
- <u>D</u>ecouple your responses from those triggers so you can manage those moments more smoothly
- <u>E</u>ngage in healthier behaviors
- <u>R</u>egulate yourself as you move forward with a new sense of awareness, realizing that you're not responsible for your partner's actions and reactions, but you are responsible for your own.

Here's Ian, using himself as an example:

IAN: *Lisa and I often end up traveling frequently for her job as a commercial director. I call us the nontourage—you know, like entourage, but not as much fun: Me, Lisa, Owen, Beckett, and our nanny all cramming into minivans and onto planes, navigating from airport to hotel and living out of wee quarters. During these times, there's little to no time for sex. Lisa's working seventeen-hour days and is so tired and consumed with the job that when she does have a shard of free time, she of course wants to spend it with the boys. Every sexual rebuff is like an arrow to the heart, and during these fragile times I take every slight offense as a cause for divorce. But once I applied my own process of reORDERing to myself, I realized some other stuff was going on beneath the surface:*

In Observing *the situation, I realized that it's more than just being sexually rebuffed, it's that I'm also being asked to go full throttle as a caretaker of the family: from doing all the driving to shopping, entertaining, and attending to the kids for fifteen hours straight. It feels like my family just keeps taking and taking from me. I start to feel like Al Pacino in* Godfather 3: *"Just when I thought I was out, they pull me back in!"*

So now personal confession: I grew up with a single mom and with a dad who was often out of the picture. I spent a lot of time having to be the adult of the house and hold down the fort. I'd always recognized myself as having developed a caretaker personality, but it wasn't until I had children that I realized just how much I resented it. I had to give to my kids what I never truly received myself in the first place. When I'm home and on my own turf in New York City, I'm able to better manage these issues, but when I'm away in a strange city, all those roiling emotions come to the surface. And they're really exacerbated by the lack of sexual/emotional connection between Lisa and me.

During the last foray of the nontourage to Los Angeles I made the concerted effort to Recognize patterns that were triggering my anger. It was mainly when Lisa was around, and even being affectionate, rather than when she was out and about, that I found myself angrily stomping around. When Lisa works there's even less time for me, and I find myself feeling even more like a third wheel. And the little dribs and drabs of affection that she is able to dole out are potent reminders of all the sustenance I'm not getting—I'm like little Oliver Twist holding out his bowl and asking for "more please." And so I made a conscious effort to Decouple the action—Lisa approaching me for a hug, or telling me how much she needs some TLC after a day on the set—from my reaction, "Well, screw off, I'm sick and tired of just taking care of people all day, what about the TLC I need?"

A hug was a really good place to start to put my new awareness into action, as opposed to tensing up or turning away, and embracing and Engaging *through the feelings until I could get to that sense of connection. It helped me to become conscious of my needs, especially when I'm traveling and intensely tending to the family. Through that insight I was able to* Regulate *my emotions and do things like take more time out of the day for myself and things like exercise that generally get pushed to the wayside.*

Ian's example is great, but we know what you're thinking: That's no fair! He's a sex therapist. How do us regular folks use this exercise? So now here is an example from Heidi's all too real life:

HEIDI: *Okay, the setup: JB and I get in a big fight about not having sex. I accuse him of sex being the only thing he cares about and not caring at all about my feelings. He accuses me of being selfish and turning my back on his needs. I take "his needs" to mean sex, which makes me more insecure and more defensive and shut him out even more. Here we go, deep breath:*

In Observing *the situation with a little care, I'm able to see that when I'm feeling overwhelmed and freaked out by something (can you say, hi new baby?) I tend to withdraw rather than ask for help or reach out for support. And withdrawing means withdrawing physically too—when I'm stressed sex is way outta my mind. When*

JB reaches out to me in the way he's most comfortable with—physically—I feel like he doesn't care about my feelings (just my super hot body thank you very much) and that freaks me out more, which makes me withdrawal more. And so on and so on.

I'm learning to Recognize this pattern about myself. When I was a kid, my parents were social activists and always busy trying to solve big world problems. When they got divorced they were even busier, figuring out their own issues and lives and big grown-up problems. I think I felt like there wasn't much room for my little kid problems. It just seemed easier to take care of myself than to ask for help or reach out for the support I needed. As a needy, sensitive kid this often left me feeling overwhelmed, scared, and alone. I still tend to withdraw rather than reach out when I'm having a hard time. But obviously, as seen above, this just makes things worse.

To De-couple my response in situations like this, I'm working on noticing when I have strong feelings of being alone. Then, instead of just going with it, the plan is to take a breath and remember I'm an adult, I'm not alone, and I've got lots of support if I can just ask for it. This means Engaging in healthier behaviors. Instead of isolating myself when I'm feeling stressed, I'm going to take a tip from Ian and force myself to reach out to JB physically with a twenty-second hug. Hopefully this will make both him and me feel more connected (and hopefully he won't take it as a come on!). Becoming aware of his love and connection will help me Regulate those old emotions and keep me a little more in the present moment—where I feel stronger, happier, and amazingly, sometimes even like reaching out sexually. Bye-bye vicious cycle! At least until the next one. . . .

Maybe all this reORDERing stuff sounds a little esoteric, and overly self-helpy, but the truth is that the ability to reappraise situations and work through them with real awareness is harder when you're a parent and in the thick of it, and all the more important when the ability to maintain an emotional connection to your partner is compromised. You don't have to be a therapist or even all that touchy-feely to take an honest look at yourself, your personal history, and the role that plays in the sexual history you're making (or not making) right now.

CHAPTER THREE

Charity Sex, Chore-play, and Other Acts of Love: When Sex Hits the Bottom of the To-do List

LIGHTS, CAMERA . . . ACTION?

Picture this: Mom and Dad sit across from each other at the dinner table, talking about the next day's plans. But it's more than dirty dishes that divides them: With the kids in bed for the night, Dad can't help but think of how long it's been since they last had sex, and how good his wife looks right now. Mom also has a faraway look as she eyes the table . . . but right now her mind is on clearing on the table as she ponders her to-do list. For Mom, sex is off the table before it even began: Foreplay has become chore-play.

Dad thinks: *I'm going to sweep all this crap off the table and take her right here and now!*

Dad says: "We haven't had sex in two and a half weeks, you know."

Mom thinks: *. . . then I'll do the dishes, then check my email and send a couple photos to my family before going to bed. In* *the morning I'll go shopping (if the baby is in a good mood) before preschool pickup. That way I can hang out with the in-laws in the afternoon before soccer and after going to the vet and still get dinner on the table. And then . . .*

Mom says: "You're an asshole."

IAN: *You know, I can't help but think the guy who speaks up about the lack of sex, and tries to initiate, is really fighting to save the relationship. Fighting for his place in the pack. He's not unlike a knight in shining armor trying to save the day.*

HEIDI: *Hmm. I don't know, maybe more like "another-night-on-the-couch-you-insensitive-cad." Maybe he's a hero for fighting to bring back the initial bond, but he's got to see that she's overwhelmed. Helping out a little more might be more the foreplay she's looking for.*

IAN: *I'm just saying that someone has to think about sex in the relationship. And fight for it. As therapist Esther Perel said, "When the father reaches out to the mother, and the mother acknowledges him, redirecting her attention, this serves to rebalance the entire family. Boundaries get drawn, and new zoning regulations get put in place delineating areas that are adult only. Time, resources, playfulness, and fun are redistributed, and libido is rescued from forced retirement. . . . The role of more autonomous parents is to help the primary caregiver disengage from the kids and reallocate energy to the couple."*

HEIDI: *But how do you "disengage" from the smell of a dirty diaper pail? The thing has got to go out, plain and simple. I promise the libido will stay at Happy Valley Libido Retirement until that happens. As for fighting for our sex lives, too often it comes out as fighting about sex.*

The sad truth of it is that complaining about not getting sex or atten-
tion does not make us want to give you sex or attention. The baby cried
all day to get our attention. Not attractive on you. Please, save the
whine for the cheese, guys. Or even better yet—bring me a glass of wine
and take out the damn diapers. Now you're talkin' dirty to me.

Sex should be fun. It should be a way to fight the disconnection that often occurs when lovers become parents. It should be pleasurable, exciting, enlightening, relieving. It should remind you why you love each other and offer a break from all things baby: a mini-spa in an otherwise overwhelming life, a respite from the drudgery of endless parenting chores. But too often, sex becomes a chore itself. It becomes something to do because you ought to, because you don't want to let someone down, because it's on your to-do list alongside fifty million other things. And if sex sometimes feels like "just another chore" to one partner, always having to be the one to initiate sex starts to feel like a responsibility to the other, which equals more stress. And even less sex. Sadly, parenting is an unromantic toe-stepper, an awkward clod of a thing slowing us all down by adding a ton of chores and minutiae to already-packed schedules. Sometimes we get so busy trying to have it all, we don't want "it" at all! With so much going on, no wonder sex is out of our minds— we're out of our minds half the time! The reality is the chores aren't just chores anymore, sex isn't just sex. It's a dance that leaves many harried parents feeling like they have four left feet.

Our children bring us joy, laughter, and awe, but they also

can bring an overwhelming, often insurmountable, sense of routine that makes us feel like we're permanently waltzing to the rhythm of "wash, rinse, repeat." Something in this shindig has got to give, and unfortunately, it's often sex and communication that go first, putting a real damper on the two-step you boogied to before. Buck up, though, because with a little instruction you'll be back out there in no time. So get your dance shoes, grab your partner, and let's get swinging again.

> I want to be able to go to bed without a sense of "having to give" my husband sex. It should be something I do for me, not just another chore.
>
> SUE, 37

> I'm constantly balancing the checkbook and thinking about what everything costs. The good news is that, hey, sex is free; the bad news is that running numbers all the time also leaves me depleted and too depressed to think about sex.
>
> BILLY, 40

CHARITY SEX, CHORE-PLAY, AND OTHER ACTS OF LOVE: WHAT MOMS WANT DADS TO KNOW
There Really Is a Connection Between Getting the Kitchen Nook Clean and Getting Nookie

> I tried to explain how exhausted and overwhelmed I felt (meanwhile, my job outside the house has also been espe-

cially busy and frantic and emotionally draining over the past week and a half), and he playfully (and with the best intentions) tried to initiate sex as a way to "relieve my stress." Oy!

SARAH, 42

I feel like I have to go through all these hoops to have her want me. Like if I do my chores and I'm a good boy, I get sex.

JON, 38

Now I'm going to tell you the real secret to turning on a mother: turning off her baby brain. Allow me to wax scientific for a moment: Researchers in the Netherlands found that "the key to female arousal seems to be deep relaxation and a lack of anxiety." In a study in which the brains of men and women were scanned during the process of sexual response using a technique called positron emission tomography (PET), the results showed that the parts of the female brain responsible for processing fear, anxiety, and emotion reduce during sexual activity. Men showed far less change in these areas of the brain. Says Dr. Gert Holstege, "What this means is that deactivation, letting go of all fear and anxiety, might be the most important thing, even necessary, to have an orgasm." So if you're a woman, getting turned on also means, ironically, letting yourself get turned off. And this means that literally, scientifically, walking past a stack of dirty dishes, or looking at an overwhelming to-do list really does turn a woman off.

Here's a recent example of mental deactivation from my life: The baby is napping. JB and I start to go at it—I'm distracted but giving it the old college try—when the dog walks in and I bust out laughing. (Note to self: Unexplained laughter in the middle of sex isn't really cool.) I try to make nice by explaining what I thought was so funny: The poor neglected dog walks in, thinking he has a good chance of going to the park since it's JB's lunch break, then sees us doing the deed and says, "guess I'm not going for a walk today." Now, it's not that funny but it gave me the giggles. I try to explain how the giggling didn't mean I wasn't into it; I just thought the dog was funny. And JB said, "Yeah, but if you were really into the sex you wouldn't have even heard the dog coming into the room." Busted.

So now you know it's true, with science and personal experience to back it up. We can't get turned on when the dog is watching us, the baby is crying, the dishes are all stacked up, dirty diapers are everywhere, something is really stinky, lunches need to be made for tomorrow, or the bills are lurking around unpaid. It's not that we require you to do these things to have sex with us, it's that we can't turn off the mom part and turn on the hot part with those things going on.

I need the stars to align, the floors clean, counters shining, and baby sleeping for me to feel even the tiniest bit aroused.

MAYA, 24

I Don't Like Being a Nag

Sometimes it's such a downer to hear what comes out of our own mouths. OMG, we sound like—ack—mothers. We say things we never thought we would say. We care about things we never thought we would care about. It's not just a hobby, not just for fun. It feels horrible to have to nag or remind you about what needs to get done. But if you don't "see" dirt, we have to point it out, and many of us don't like it. It makes us feel like we have another kid, not a partner. It makes us not like you so much, and when we don't like you so much, we don't like having sex with you so much. Men need to get this and help with chores more—without being asked. Women don't want to feel like they have to ask or, worse, say "hooray" every time you do something around the house. After all, you live there too! Yes, some guys have a steeper learning curve than others when it comes to the "home arts," but really, I don't know a woman who just natu-rally *loves* the smell of dirty diapers! The sad un-PC truth of things is that a common complaint Ian hears in his practice (and I hear at the playground, so it must be true) is that women feel they bear the majority of the burden for household chores. Even if we work, most of us come home to a second shift of cleaning, cooking, and chaos. So if you want to see more hottie and less harpy, make sure those chores are done. Think of it this way: If you do a chore, that right there saved precious physical and emotional energy we can share with you in other ways.

Lately, every time I turn on the TV it seems as if there is a sitcom with a fat, balding, eternally adolescent man and his "uptight," out of his league, skinny saint of a wife. Those shows might as well all be called *The Bitch and the Giant Baby*. Now, I have no problem with overweight or balding men, but I really have a problem with glamorizing men who can barely wipe their own butts. It's not cute. It just makes us pissed. After all, we'd love an extended adolescence too! We don't like worrying about everything, knowing the details of mercury in fish and vaccines and the poop schedules of our kids. It's not fun, but when you don't step up and proactively take some of this stuff on it only makes things worse, forcing us into bitch/baby mode, which frankly is a lot funnier on TV than in real life.

I want to do the right thing . . . just the easiest right thing.

CHUCK, 37

Sometimes True Charity Begins in Bed . . .

Sometimes we just can't turn it all off and get turned on. But sometimes we find we have the opportunity and at least slight inclination to make sex happen. So we do. While often called "pity sex," there is a time and place for sex getting done just to get it done. I know, I know. Romantic, right? JB calls pity sex "corpse sex" or "Real Dolling." I remember when we first heard about those $7,000 lifelike, orifice-correct Real Dolls all those years ago, we lay in bed in our funky little apartment laughing, trying to imagine what kind of loser would need to get it on with a vinyl doll instead of a real person. We were so full of hormones and ourselves and each other we couldn't imagine the wrinkly horror of a future like that.

Fast-forward, though, to the months following the birth of our daughter, and there I was, often my husband's very own Real Doll, barely lifelike myself, letting him essentially masturbate inside me so I could cross sex off my list and get back to what really mattered—like the dishes.

To me there is a difference between what we're calling a pity fuck and true charity sex. While they are close cousins, there are some fundamental differences. Pity sex is a problem for those of us with easily lost or misplaced libidos because it's *bad* sex—and bad sex is bad news for the libido because it doesn't inspire a whole lot of anticipation. But charity sex can be quite nice. If pity sex is all about checking something off the list, true charity sex is all about checking in. It's not about meeting someone else's physical needs—it's about meeting your relationship's emotional ones. It's about opening up, quite literally, to each other.

I feel like I do so much that goes unrecognized—don't guys deserve a little respect too?

WILLIAM, 34

Okay, guys. We know you've given up a lot lately: lazy football Sundays, lazy college football Saturdays, lazy high school football Friday nights . . . but seriously, with the baby we're both working harder than ever, every spare moment now goes to cleaning up poop or playing peekaboo. Gone are fun nights and leisurely mornings in bed—we miss those too, even if it doesn't seem like it sometimes. We know you work hard, at work and at home, and that you do all kinds of things to keep our family running smoothly.

We love watching you with the kids, and we know you'd bite off your own arm in an instant to keep us all safe and sound, if you needed to. We are so thankful you're our own personal tech guy, our exterminator, and our dog poop patrol dude. We might get frustrated and wish you'd do more around the house, but we really are grateful for that stuff. We also know there is tons of stuff we don't see that you do, and we love you for it. And we probably don't say it enough. So thank you thank you thank you. We love you we love you we love you.

CHARITY SEX, CHORE-PLAY, AND OTHER ACTS OF LOVE: WHAT DADS WANT MOMS TO KNOW
Keep the Appreciation Comin'

As a dad/husband this last paragraph makes me want to cry. So often moms seem to get instant membership to the "I don't know how she does it" club. Yes, moms should be revered, appreciated, granted instant martyrdom for being a mom. You're awesome, and exhausted. But you're not the only one doing a million and one things. We're tired too. We're overwhelmed too. And while it's now kind of culturally cool for moms to "tell the truth" or bitch about the realities of motherhood, dads haven't really gotten the same pass yet.

It's hard to admit that parenting can be mind-crushing and soul-depleting for us. It's just so culturally anathema to stand up and say, "This sucks." Not all the time, but some of the time, and clearly enough of the time to keep those statistics about one out of two marriages ending in divorce roughly accurate. This chapter is all about chores, but really a chore is just a subunit of an overall routine that can strip the life out of life, even while life is blossoming around us. We need to take some of that mindfulness medicine as well, to practice putting everything aside and allowing ourselves to really experience the joy of the moment. These really are the best days of our lives, but sometimes we just need a reminder to actually feel it.

In our relationships, it's too easy to get caught up in a game of "who does more" or "who's more tired/overworked/ stressed." But there are no winners in that one. Why not skip it and take the high road instead? Every time you find yourself feeling in need of appreciation, reach out and give some instead. You just might be surprised at the results.

> My therapist is always telling me to learn to live in the moment, and I want to shout, "Dude, I'm squeezing every ounce of life out of a free moment that I can—I'm stepping on those moments like little grapes I'm trying to make wine from—I can totally live in the moment, there just aren't enough free moments to actually live in.
>
> FRANK, 38

I'm Up At Night Too . . . And Maybe Not As Up As I Once Was . . .

Maybe it's a function of how dads are genetically wired, but I know I can't look into my children's little eyes without seeing visions of college tuitions, spring breaks, trips abroad, and the little Picasso who's going to grow up to be a starving artist. Even if it's years away, it feels like it's right around the corner. The sense of long-term pressure and responsibility keeps many of us dads up at night, and maybe not so "up" when we should be. As a result, many new fathers find themselves dealing with low desire, or even their first bouts of erectile issues. Getting/maintaining an erection can prove challenging when a guy feels overwhelmed by life. If this happens, don't take it personally. Lots of women jump to the conclusion that if a guy doesn't want to have sex, or can't maintain an erection, that it must be a function of her desirability. But often, as with you, it's just the stuff outside the bedroom that's seeping its way into our love life.

Speaking of outside-the-bedroom stuff, I'm definitely also one of those guys that has a hard time chilling out if there's a sink full of dishes, a hamper full of laundry, or a desk splattered with bills. While Lisa is bathing the boys, I'm usually cleaning and picking up around the house, and our respective chores never seem to end. The chore zone is 6 to 10 p.m., and there's no way I could even really think about sex knowing that the dishwasher needs to be emptied and then refilled, or there's some lingering utility bill awaiting payment. I think where it's different is by the time we actually get to the point where we're possibly having sex—if we get to that point—I'm totally gung ho, no mental deactivation required, whereas Lisa's mind is still racing. Lisa and I seem to be on different anxiety schedules: I can't think about anything when I'm submerged in the chore zone other than what's the next thing that needs to be done, and Lisa can't turn off the noise once it's actually off.

I'd Rather Walk 500 Miles to Go Buy Diapers Than Actually Change One

It's easy for us guys to get so worn out by routine that an overwhelming sense of anxiety, restlessness, and claustrophobia settle in, which can lead to a pretty bummed out baby state of mind. Sometimes the answer is as simple as getting out of the house to run an errand. These days guys can't turn on the TV or open up a magazine without hearing about the supersensitive stay-at-home dad who loves nothing more than watching the Wiggles and changing diapers. But for many of us, child care can be monotonous and the walls start to come in on us. But give us something to do that takes us out in the world and we're more than happy to do it.

Okay, before Heidi wallops my pathetic burnt-out brain with a sidebar about how child care is not an acquired taste for women either and that guys need to get up off their lazy inept asses and just show some &*&^%^% initiative, let me apologize now for any moronic gender stereotyping and rest my already lost case on the not so infamous "poop test," in which thirteen mothers were asked to sniff dirty diapers belonging to both their own child as well as other babies. According to the researchers who conducted the study and then published the results in the *Journal of Evolution and*

Human Behavior, mothers consistently rated the smell of their own child's diapers as less disgusting than those of the other babies. The researchers opined that this response is quite possibly a function of evolutionary design: "A mother's disgust at her baby's feces has the potential to obstruct her ability to care for her baby and may even affect the strength of the bond she has with her baby."

Okay, admittedly this study demonstrates very little about the general female disposition toward child care, and conducting a study with thirteen women is hardly a universal sample. (Although, Lisa did tell me she's not at all bothered by the smell of Beckett and Owen's poop, so I guess that's fourteen.) But give a guy a choice between sniffing a diaper (or changing one for that matter) and going out in the middle of a snowstorm, hell even a hurricane, to buy one, and we'll gladly return with some Huggies and a six-pack of Bud Light.

If I May: Heidi

Ian, you knew this one was coming . . . so let me keep it short: I know my daughter's poop stinks. I've known it since the first jar of peas was introduced (breast milk poops don't count . . . everyone, even JB, olfactory oaf that he is, knows breast milk poop smells like microwave popcorn. Good? Bad? Judge for yourself.) But these food poops really are quite foul. So study debunked right there, dude! So guys, you are certainly welcome to go get us beer, just prepare to change a diaper when you get back. And personally, I prefer Corona.

No One Likes a Martyr: Ian

Got it, Heidi. Of course, the household help advice cuts both ways. It's important to resist being the martyr because you're the only one who can do it right. Men are not mind readers! If you need help or you're feeling overwhelmed, can you please just say, "take the garbage out" or "help me now"? Enough with the "meta messages" already. Tell us what you really want —what's really going on—and we'll most likely do it. Even if we're not happy about it, we'll be happier than trying to figure out why you're pissed at us later.

If you're constantly telling us we don't clean well enough, or you change the baby's clothes out of the random stripes/polka dot thing we chose this morning when you think we're not looking, we're going to lose the incentive to help. Communicate with us, show us how you would like it done—then think about letting go a little. If you want a real partner, don't treat us like babies. Ask for help if you need it and do it in a way that's nice and to the point. Chances are, we'll be receptive and you'll wonder why you didn't do it ages ago.

And please, keep in mind: sometimes messy can be good. Sloppy can be sexy. I know you're thinking this sounds crazy, but maybe what we need is a little mess, a little clutter in our lives, and I'm not talking about dirty dishes. I'm talking about in the rhythm of our life. Now that we're parents, everything is wearing down to a routine. Why did we bother with wedding vows? We should have just read our respective to-do lists. Right now life seems like one big giant chore, with lots of much smaller chores. We're chores within a chore, so let's mess things up a little, let's embrace some clutter, let's get it on in dirty sheets. What the hell?

Please Chill Out

As you now know, stress and anxiety actually make it impossible for a woman to relax and enjoy sex. And when they're in full-on mommy mode, unfortunately, many of you know stress, anxiety, and fear all too well. Historically this "on alert" status served a purpose—keeping saber-toothed tigers from eating their young. While you don't have the same risks you had living in the wild, in the spirit of adaptation, you've probably found plenty of new things to obsess about (SIDS, falls, fevers, choking, illness, accidents, tap water, immunizations, head size, body size, preschool, college . . . you get the picture). The next time you find yourself worrying about baby related business, check yourself. Is this something you really have control over? Have you done everything in your ability to handle the situation?

If so, step back, take a breath and try to trust the universe and let go. It's scary, and it's hard, but it's a baby step in a process that will continue on for the next, oh, twenty-five years or so. The good news? It gets easier as they get older. The really good news? Once you're able to turn that stuff off, during orgasm the female brain's emotion centers shut down, producing an almost trance like state. So it's time to start thinking of sex again as a much-needed break. It's time to start enjoying sex again for some much needed recreation—not just procreation.

Having Sex with Me to Cross It Off Your To-do List Bums Me Out

She would do it with me, but only out of guilt. Totally uninspired. It was more like necrophilia, really.

DAVIS, 38

While I have to say most of us guys would agree that pity sex is better than no sex, it's really a bummer to have sex with someone not because they're hot and heavy for you but because their to-do list is getting heavy and they need to cross something off it, or like sex is something we get if we're good boys. The thing is, anticipation is the jump-start for stalled sexuality. It's the sublime fuel that turns even the tiniest spark of a sexy thought into an explosion. But what's to anticipate when it comes to pity sex? The physical disassociation? That thousand-mile stare? The dull resentment and suspicion that the supernova that was once your sex life is now entering the dreary slow fade department?

We want you to have sex with us because you want us, not because we took out the garbage. In the same way whining about sex makes you feel like it's just about sex rather than being about "sex with you," treating sex like a chore makes a guy feel as important and significant as a dirty diaper. We don't want your pity, we want *you*.

My annual New Year's resolution is to "have more sex with my husband," right under the "be a better wife" category.

MARY, 33

AND A WORD ABOUT THAT GUILT, LADIES

For some reason, mothering and guilt seem to go hand in hand. While guilt is helpful sometimes to let us know when things in our life are out of whack, women, particularly mothers, often take it too far. Thanks in large part to unrealistic societal expectations, these days mothers have guilt about so much. About working . . . or not working. For taking time for yourselves, . . . or not taking enough time for yourselves. Shoot, some mothers feel guilty about feeling guilty! The problem is that guilt and sexy feelings just don't mix. So whether you're feeling guilty because you want to do something really *freaky* in the sack, or because you'd rather sack out, it's time to take a breath and *let it go* . . . guilt free. Here's a word we want you to use at least once a day: "No." As in, "No, I can't do that favor for you," or "No, that won't work," or even, "No, I don't want to make love tonight." It's okay, it won't kill anyone. But learning to say no just might help you to say yes to other good stuff in life. Including more sex.

SEX RX FOR THE LADIES: GET YOURSELF A PIECE OF MIND(FULNESS)

If the key to getting and staying turned on is peace of mind, the practice of mindfulness might be just the hobby to help us start feeling like getting more of a piece of . . . ass. What is mindfulness? It just means paying attention to what's going on right now—being aware of the present moment. In life, and particularly in parenting, it's so easy to get caught up in the future (i.e., worrying or planning) or caught in the past (i.e., wishful regrets or blaming) that we're not really here 100 percent. We give our kids time outs to help ground them and bring them back to reality when they're freaking out, but we rarely do the same. Taking the time to be here, now, can make us better parents and better lovers. We have to be here—not a million miles away on the stress bus careening out of control—but here, fully present and sane with our kids. Similarly, we need to be grounded in the moment, and ourselves, before we can enjoy and share those selves with another person (in bed).

You don't need Enya or incense, or even a quiet place to practice mindfulness. In fact, it's probably most helpful to you in those times you feel most hectic—running errands, dealing with the kids, whenever, wherever. Taking a minute or two to be mindful and gather yourself can help. A good place to start is with your body:

Pay attention to your breath when you're frustrated, or

just whenever you think of it throughout the day. Focus on feeling the air coming in and out of your nose.

When you're standing, take a minute to notice your feet on the ground. Really try to feel them touching the ground. When your mind wanders, and it will, take a breath and start over again until you really start to feel grounded. Wash. Rinse. Repeat as needed.

SEX RX FOR THE GUYS: GET UP, SHOW UP

As parents, half the battle is showing up. Guys tend to check out on this more than their partners. As Ian admits, "I know I do a lot of things in a half-assed, careless way, and it's usually the stuff I should be putting my heart and soul into: telling Owen a halfway interesting story at bedtime, and not one that has more pauses than a Pinter play; actually brushing Beckett's teeth without thinking to myself, these are just baby teeth, how clean do they really need to be; hugging Lisa and actually making a connection instead of feeling like she's the traffic cop that just pulled me over for no reason at all on my way to an important meeting." At one point in our lives, didn't we get graded on effort? Let's pretend we're there again. Stop grading yourself on a curve and aim for a genuine A. Show up and do your share, every day, all the way. You might be surprised at the rewards.

TO DO TOGETHER: (DON'T) DIVIDE AND CONQUER

Sure it's easier to do a diaper run and pay the bills while she bathes and does the night-night routine with the little one, but this divide and conquer routine often conquers your libidos. Do more together, even if it means getting less done. Instead of conquering and dividing our way down the task list, let's meander and unite. In a time of multitasking, maybe we need to do more of these chores and the daily drudgery together. From cooking and cleaning up together to bathing the kids, chores don't have to lead to isolation. Tonight: Everyone cleans up after dinner together.

IN CONCLUSION

The votes are in! The brain really is the biggest sex organ—and now it's time to start appreciating it as such. Let's give it a rest now and then, let's let it cut loose and check out (in a good way) for a while. The survival work of having small children can be tedious and consume every inch of free mind space. Beyond that, your chores really have increased as well, causing a new level of routine and desire-crushing banality. It's easy to let little resentments about workload build up to the point where that's all we can see—resentment. We stop seeing them as sexy and fun and start seeing them as giant babies instead, another gropy lil' person needing something from us! But keeping a running list of tit for tat, (or tit for tit)—whether it's who did what in the kitchen, the office, the nursery, or the sack—is a zero sum game. After all, how do you quantify breast-feeding? Is a late-night diaper change worth three take-out-the-garbage points? There's no correct equation for connection. Without actively shifting gears and priorities, sex will keep getting lodged in the brain as another must-do, rather than a woo-hoo-we-get-to-do.

The superparent mind is a scary place—a jungle of to-do jingle jangle, a mass of multitasking monsters popping up and sending you on a white-knuckle trip. But you've got to make sure you take time to enjoy the ride, and ride each other. You've got to slow down and be here in the moment—as a lover, a parent, or just a human being looking for sanity. Giving sex a real shot is not about checking something off the list, it's about checking in with each other. It's about leaving the dishes and the kids and all that crap and giving yourself over to a moment of time and space together. Nobody is giving, nobody is taking, but everybody is sharing. It's not easy, but with a little tenderness (and in less time than the standard pity fuck) you can find yourself in a beautiful, charitable moment where two separate people actually feel like one. Now that's something worth anticipating.

CHAPTER FOUR

When the TV Is Turned on More Than You: Or Why Your Libido Is a Function of Your Lifestyle

LIGHTS, CAMERA . . . ACTION?

Picture this: Mom and Dad climb into bed for the night, well covered in baby-weight-hiding flannel and a bag of chips between them. "We should really have sex one of these days," says Mom, as she pops some chips and replaces the batteries in her trusty . . . remote.

"Yep, we should," says Dad, chewing. "Should I warm up some more spicy cheese sauce?" He adds to the romance by reaching for the nightstand and pulling out . . . his laptop. He turns on his screen, she turns on hers, and just like that they are both turned off.

IAN: *Ah, yes, nachos instead of nookie—I know it well. I've been through two sympathetic pregnancies and still haven't lost my baby weight.*

HEIDI: *JB's favorite joke, while carrying the baby and lagging behind me on walks, is to say, "Hey, hold up there, I've got twenty extra pounds here . . . plus the baby!" He consoled himself during my pregnancies by having late-night three-ways with his friends Ben and Jerry.*

IAN: *And tortilla chips aren't the only passion killers in the above scene: An Italian study found that couples with TVs in the bedroom had about half as much sex as those without one.*

HEIDI: *So let me guess—you've got to turn it off to turn things on?*

IAN: *You got it.*

Okay, so we now all know that the brain really is our biggest sex organ (and that a clean house truly is an aphrodisiac). But sexual excitement doesn't stop there. The brain can get wooed all it wants, but if those thoughts get lost in the body, well, what's the point? The fact of the matter is that there is a strong physical component to sexual health. For both men and women, sexual health and overall health are intimately connected. So if your idea of exercise is getting up to change the channel, or you're still wearing your maternity pants (but they're so comfy . . .) and your kid is four, this chapter is for you. It's time to strip off the excuses and start taking care of yourself—with at least as much care as you give to everyone else. Because, if you're not taking time to physically rejuvenate yourself, you're not going to get too far sexually rejuvenating yourself either.

One of the biggest complaints Ian hears from couples is that one or both of them has "let themselves go" and no longer cares about looking attractive to the other. While "letting go" is definitely a skill you'll need in parenting, this kind of "letting go" is not what we're talking about. Letting yourself go often means you've given up on sex—you stop thinking about it as much, stop wanting it as much, and stop trying as hard to get it. It also too often means giving up on you—as a whole, happy, healthy person. Yes, in the daily grind of parenting it's easy to put yourself last on the list. But now is when you need it the most. After all, how can you keep from snapping and snickering at your loved ones when the Snickers bar you had for breakfast causes a major crash by lunchtime? How can you feel like an Energizer Bunny in the sack when you've gorged yourself on the Easter Bunny's leftovers? It may seem like you don't have time or energy for eating right or exercise, but working that self-care into your life is not only good for your long-term health, it pays off in the short term too with more energy, sounder sleep (for what little sleep you do get), feeling better in your body, and just plain enjoying yourself in bed and out.

This chapter is not about guilting you into losing the baby weight or sending any more unrealistic body images your way—there are plenty of those out there. Particularly with the beautiful people baby bump phenomenon—but those beautiful people also have beautiful trainers to help them lose the postpartum bump. The rest of us, not so much. But it is about inspiring you to not give up on yourself, or You—as a Sexual Person. The verdict is in. Sex is good for you.

Sex . . .

1. Boosts your immune system to help fight off colds—and
    hey, you've been getting those a lot lately, especially if you
    go anywhere near a preschool. Weekly sex is known to
    boost immunoglobulin, so forget an apple a day, and go
    for an orgasm a day.
2. Burns calories: You've heard it, it's true—some good
    basic sex is going to burn about 200 calories if you
    go at it for about half an hour. If you happen to be
    breast-feeding, a sex/breast-feeding regime will keep
    you 1,000 calories ahead of the game before you even
    think about exercise.
3. Works as a facial—and we don't mean the kind you find in
    a porno. One study in Edinburgh took a group of judges
    and asked them to look at a group of women through a
    one-way mirror, and then guess their ages. The women
    who had sex regularly (we're talking a few times a week)
    were consistently thought to look ten or so years younger
    than their actual age. The researchers opined that sex
    raises estrogen levels, which contributes to shiny lustrous
    hair and good skin.
4. Helps with headaches, and not just the kind you use as an
    excuse not to have sex. Orgasms have an analgesic affect,
    which soothes headaches and general pain.
5. Strengthens pelvic floor muscles. Forget kegels, or better
    yet flex your kegels while you're having sex and go for
    some real vaginal strength training.

So let's get healthy and get it on!

I self-diagnosed my condition as "why-bother-I'll-just-wear-sweatpants-for-the-twentieth-time-in-a-row-syndrome."

LESLIE, 28

I had no way of explaining to my husband exactly what the hell was happening to my body.

ALIX, 32

THE TV IS TURNED ON MORE THAN YOU: WHAT MOMS WANT DADS TO KNOW
I Sure Don't Feel Hot ...

It's rough getting used to our new bodies. We've gained a lot of . . . wisdom over the past year(s) and have a lot of extra . . . smarts to show for it. While I personally haven't had trouble losing most of my pregnancy weight, that doesn't account for the way things have shifted around on me. Things are just proportioned differently—they hang funny. And thanks to huge boobs, I look bigger, even though technically I weigh about the same as I did pre-babies. We are not only contending with fussy bodies, but also the fickle images society has about what a sexy woman looks like.

News flash, guys, we don't look like that. We've never looked like that and never will. It might be time to get a reality check about what to expect from us. We are real, not airbrushed. We don't have personal trainers, we have potty training. And though that involves lots of sprinting and squatting, it doesn't equal an instant hot bod, which we may never have even had in the first place. New moms used to get a free pass from all the media images that celebrate anorexic bodies. But with the sexualization of pregnancy and the boom in celebrity babies, these days there's more pressure than ever on moms to look good, fast. Guys, this is the time for you to step up and help us appreciate our bodies in a way we might be stuck at right now. It's time to remind us that sexy is not about what our body looks like but how we use it. Please note that this is definitely not the time to introduce some mirror or video play. It's time for strategic lighting and blanket use. It's time to worship us *as is*, and love it (or fake it pretty damn well if you don't).

. . . Though I Am Kind of Bothered

So what's up with the "hot mom" trend these days? It seems as if everywhere I look in the media these days there's a hot mom who looks great and appears to be having a smokin' sex life. Sure, they're bouncing off the walls on Wisteria Lane like it's nothing, but let's get real: A lot of us have to actually work at it. The reality is, sexuality doesn't exist in a vacuum. It's not just what we look like that makes us feel sexy or not. There are other things at play here. The media plays a role. Workplace attitudes play a role. (Hot: more "career carousel" flexibility. Not: pumping in the bathroom.) Society plays a role. (Hot: universal health care, excellent schools, Social Security, and tax breaks for years spent caring for other people—young or old. Not: worrying, overstretching, worrying, overstretching, worrying.) And, of course, our partners play a significant role. (Hot: sex when I like my husband. Not: sex when I don't.)

My point is, I think it's much easier for us to explore our inner hotties when we have some help. I feel most sexy when I like my body and my life, when I'm not stressed about money or child care or work, when I feel strong and supported. Since as a society we're still working on getting past MILF contests and into real mother love, I shoot small. Rather than seeking mythical "hot mom" status, I tend to go for "hot moments" instead.

My favorite way, these days, to create a little personal heat is to start wet. I crank the shower to hot. The sting of the heat melts my mom skin and gets my blood flowing. I waste water. I lather up with body wash that's not baby-scented or berry-scented. I appreciate my body the way the media never will, the way my husband does, like something precious in its imperfection. I stay in there, alone, until I'm almost dizzy with heat, drunk with uninterrupted me time. In a perfect hot moment, the baby is asleep and my daughter is being cared for elsewhere, leaving me free to step out of the shower and flop down naked on the bed, steaming, overheated, pulsing. I rest on crisp sheets wondering when JB will find me, and when he does I tell him I'm resting, I'm napping, I'm asleep, I'm too hot and too tired and too overworked to move so I just might have to lie there while he takes advantage of me. Which he usually does. And before I know it my body starts generating an altogether new kind of heat.

Let's Get Physical

Physical activity gets blood flowing . . . to all areas of the body if you know what we mean. Blood flow = better sex. Energy = better sex. Feeling better about our bodies = better sex. If that's not enough reason to get walking, remember that exercise can also fight off the Big D, depression—and not being depressed = better sex. Sounds good, right? But why is it so hard? Since you guys are not exactly spring chickens either, how 'bout we start a little exercise plan together? Help us by turning evening walks into a family routine and committing to an exercise program with us. Having a life that includes exercise takes more than just plain old motivation—it takes planning, child care, and encouragement. We just might need a swift kick in the butt to actually get off ours and make it happen. The best approach? Model it for us. And don't forget to remind us just how many calories we burn each time we get it on.

One of the most romantic things JB does is go hiking with me. (Sexy, right? No, but it is.) He's not a big nature guy (read: allergies), but he toughs it out for me. He knows that when I get out there, where it's quiet and still and beautiful, I come to life. I start feeling things I bury in the grind of getting through the day, I start opening up to the world and sensations and yes . . . wait for it guys . . . opening up to him, in a sexual way. He loves that he can do this for me, and he also loves the idea of other hikers stumbling upon us while we're getting busy with the bees. He doesn't love, so much, the poison oak part of it.

Sometimes I'm Just Hungry and Tired . . .
or Maybe Just Constipated

**My body has been through the ringer. Unfortunately for my
husband, I often feel it has become a no-man's land.**

TIFFANY, 22

A person really only has so much energy. A woman can survive only so long on Goldfish and caffeine. Beyond that, breast-feeding has us putting out all those extra calories. Even if we're not breast-feeding, we're still chasing kids around, not sleeping well at night, and generally burning the candle at both ends. As time goes on, people stop doting on us, bringing us glasses of water, and leaving meals on the steps, and we're on our own. This can leave us cranky, and not feeling sexy. Help us out here. Make sure we're taking our vitamins. Put food and water in front of us.

We also might feel fat or worry about being able to lose weight so we're starving ourselves, and then bingeing because we're hungry. Get the whole house on a healthy diet that includes lots of fruits and vegetables, as well as plenty of protein for stamina. And definitely include fiber since constipation is an issue for many moms—after all, who wants to add more cars when the train is already having trouble leaving the track?

And speaking of feeling hungry, go ahead and add some meat to the menu . . . if your lady finds she's craving it. No, I don't work for the cattle lobbyists (in fact I only recently started eating meat again when I was pregnant), but I swear there's a correlation between meat and wanting sex! I was keeping track of any time I had a little libido surge or had sex, and lo and behold, seven out of ten times it happened after eating meat.

Before we all run out and carnivore it up, though, let me point out that I usually only eat meat when I'm out at a restaurant, so sure, it could have to do with other factors. I don't have to cook while the baby's at my breast and my seven-year-old is whining. We were out on a date, away from the kids, and wine was involved . . . but still it makes me wonder. If you find yourself craving the actual meat more than the night out, make sure you're getting enough iron (many women are low) and vitamin B12, especially for you veggies out there.

Self-Medicating Just Ain't Cool

Watch out, dads. We might be tempted to turn into one of those hip mamas who sneaks out for a smoke, has cocktails at four in the afternoon because you-know-how-parenting-can-be, and schedules Prosecco playdates. It's not just that smoking and drinking give us a way of "treating ourselves," of giving ourselves a little something in the middle of all this to help us feel good, though that's certainly a part of it. (Imagine if our kids took care of themselves that way, though: *Mommy, this teething thing is a drag. I'll be outside in my ExerSaucer smokin' a fattie.* Nice.) It's also that we're trying to prove (probably more to ourselves than to you or anybody else) that by drinking or smoking we're more than the sweatpants-wearin', kid-corallin' lady everyone else sees at Kid's Club. We're with the program, we're bad ass, we're young and plenty naughty still. Right? Please? Believe me, I know the drill, I have the sweatpants to prove it.

But how about this? How about we ditch the dirty habits together and pick up some new ones instead? That way, the next time one of us wants to prove we're not nearly as stuffy as the new minivan smell you know we're both wearing, we can let a set of padded handcuffs fall out of your pants pocket. *Whoops, silly me. It's just been that kind of day and I can hardly wait to get home and fuck my brains out . . .* now that's what I'm talking about. We need to develop some naughty habits again that are naughty in only the healthiest of ways. Help us be the kind of mom that "accidentally" shows off our new mini-vibrator while digging through our purse for a Hello Kitty Band-Aid. *Hip Mama Ladies*, we'll tell our friends, with a knowing look, *you know how it is after a long day with the kids and you just want to let loose and get your rocks off*. Oh yeah. Now that's real self-care, baby. The kind best done with a loving partner's support. And before you know it, once again we'll both be too cool for preschool. Without all those pesky carcinogens.

Don't Underestimate Hormones, Like, Ever

No one ever told me just how powerful estrogen is.

BETSY, 39

Ah, hormones. Where to begin. While often blamed excessively, right now hormones should always be high on the list of suspects. Sex drive is directly related to hormones—for both men and women. So they can mess up both your mood and your mmmrrraoww. There's a line in the movie *Knocked Up*, where a guy and his pregnant girlfriend are fighting. Frustrated, he finally yells, "I know this is just your hormones talking, but—FUCK YOU, HORMONES!" That's the truth. Take a woman's normal mood swings and multiply that by one million and you've got the postpartum thing dialed. Often it's best just to ride things out and get the heck out of the way, but occasionally, like if we're really abnormally up, down, or tired, it might be time to push us to see a doctor.

For some women, levels of thyroid hormones drop too much after giving birth. (The thyroid is a small gland in the neck that helps to regulate your metabolism.) Low thyroid levels can cause symptoms like feeling depressed or irritable, fatigue, difficulty concentrating, sleep problems, and weight gain. Of course, as we mentioned in Chapter 2, postpartum depression can cause those things too. There's a lot of overlap here. The takeaway point is that if we're acting crazy it might be nice to point it out to us in a gentle, kind way—or maybe over the phone, just to be safe. But it's not necessarily a character flaw in us—we just might be at the mercy of a larger force . . . like hormones.

THE TV IS TURNED ON MORE THAN YOU: WHAT DADS WANT MOMS TO KNOW

You're Hot

You don't know how often we just look at you across the room and suddenly a little Billy Crystal pops into our head and says, "You look marvelous." Not to mention hot. We know you think we're crazy: How can we possibly think you look sexy when you feel overweight and out of shape, when you haven't had time to work out, and when your clothes are all poop- and puke-stained and you haven't showered in two days? We get it. But you know what? We still think you're hot. Not to say that you don't look great after spending three hours primping and preening for the dinner party we don't want to go to. But that moment when you just bent down to put the dishes in the dishwasher? Your butt looked awesome! That moment when you threw on jeans and a ratty T-shirt to go answer the door? You were smoking.

Call us crazy, but hey, there's a guy inside this dad. We still think about sex at least a hundred times a day, and no one makes us think about it more than you. Sometimes you get so down on yourself or focused on "looking desirable" that you forget to study what really makes you feel desirable, what really gets you going as opposed to what you think gets us going. Look at your body—it's awesome. It's a window into a sense-based life, senses beyond calendula cream and Burt's Bees for Babies. You've forgotten all that it can do for you— run, swim, dance, make love, play with the kids . . . heck, play with yourself! When's the last time you did that? The point is, your body is a temple and frankly, you've been neglecting it. Take a belly dancing class or spend the darn money and do that yoga baby class. Believe us, we're willing to support you if it will support sex!

> All I have to do is hug my husband and he gets hard. Well, it's my body that's making him hard. It's his eyes he sees me with. He still loves me. And he still wants me.
>
> CHANTAL, 40

That Said, Truth Be Told, You're, Er, Looking a Little Less Hot to Us

Any guy who's been through the trenches of sex and relationship knows to smile and keep his big mouth shut when he hears the question, "Do I look fat?" And many men are more turned on by imperfect women who let their inner hotties shine, despite what's going on on the outside. But while a little confidence can go a long way, "weighty" matters should not always be treated lightly.

I've had numerous sessions with couples stuck in a rut who spend countless hours and dollars opining about why they're no longer feeling sexual when in truth they are feeling sexual, they're just not attracted to their partner. That might sound a little harsh, but it can be a reality. Of course, so is the reality of being a woman; bodies change, especially in pregnancy, and expecting your wife to look like Heidi Klum is a recipe for disaster. Let's remember, supermodels get paid to look like supermodels, and supermoms have to squeeze in sit-ups between poopy diapers and spit ups! But I do think we can't just brush it under the rug. So let's get a little advice from the ladies on this one. So, Heidi, what's the best way for a guy to let his lady know he's less attracted to her?

HEIDI: *Yikes, Ian. I don't really want to touch this with a ten-foot pole, but here goes: I would say that it's highly likely the woman is well aware of the problem, unless she lives in some sort of alternate universe. She might, however, be much less aware of how to actually do something about it. Offering concrete things such as: "I'll take the kids every Tuesday and Thursday night so you can go work out," shows real support. Get the whole family walking in the evenings, offer to do the shopping and get only healthy stuff, cook more—and present her with healthy meals. Similarly, phrasing things in a positive way that shows love and support should be more productive. For instance, compare "I just don't find you attractive anymore" with "I want you to be healthy," or even "Let's both get back into shape. What can we do?" I have to say I'm also a little wary, though, of guys using pregnancy weight as an excuse for other reasons they're not attracted. Maybe it knocks the woman off her pedestal a bit, makes her a real person instead of the image of woman and mother out there. Maybe it's more that she's not as playful or naughty as she once was, or energetic. I'm not saying that guys shouldn't be put off by extra weight, but beware it's not something else either. The sad truth is that parenthood makes it easy to let ourselves go—we're so immersed in parenting culture, so stressed out and worried for our kids and* *their future that we often quite literally let our "selves" go. We sink so deep into our roles as parents that we forget the selves we had before—selves that played and flirted, that were interesting and exciting, that used to primp properly and not take each other for granted so much. So while I'm generally put off by the concept of "he really let himself go" in terms of reflecting on what kind of human being someone is, I think there is validity to it in terms of looking at what we've given up for parenthood. I'm not talking about giving up like giving up the freedom to go get a drink when we want, or eat what we want without ever paying for it! I'm talking about giving up on the idea that there is more to us than mother or father, more to us than diaper changer or disciplinarian.*

IAN: *Right on, Heidi. So the real takeaway here is to support each other. Helping your spouse find parts of him- or herself that have fallen by the wayside—including exercising and eating right—is a way better project to take on together than a simple weight loss program for one of you.*

I'm Not Exactly Loving My Body Either

What can I say? I am so not fit to fuck.

JOEL, 42

It's unfair. Admittedly we didn't go through the process of childbirth, but after delivery you quickly lose some of the weight and we stay fat. With both of Lisa's pregnancies, I gained weight right along with her. And just when I got down to my ideal weight after a year of dieting, the whole thing happened all over again. I would look at pictures of me and my sons, and I looked bloated. I didn't even notice the smiles of my kids in the photos; all I could focus on was my fat face. I also wasn't interested in sex. I just didn't feel sexual. Sure, I was often too full from eating, or lethargic from the lack of exercise, but my self-esteem was at an all-time low. I also was mad at Lisa for giving herself a pregnancy "free pass" on whatever she wanted to eat: nachos at bedtime, cold pizza for breakfast, an explosion of colorful cupcakes from the Magnolia bakery, midnight taco runs. My life became a page out of *Fast Food Nation*.

Even if you say we look fine, that we're cute, weight gain and low self-esteem can still make us feel out of sorts. And that easily carries over into the bedroom. Help us in the same way we can help you. Support eating right and getting exercise. In men, excess body fat increases estrogen levels, which could have the effect of decreasing testosterone. So we could use some help with our diet. Also, encourage us to hit the gym and lift some weights. Building muscle mass requires testosterone and experts say that compound exercises that hit many muscle groups such as squats and bench-presses boost t-levels. After this last pregnancy, Lisa both inspired and led by example: bringing healthy foods and snacks back into the house, losing weight herself and staying fit. I told myself I'm not going to let Lisa be the only fit one here, and I treated it as a challenge.

ED and PE Are Not "Education" and "Phys. Ed"

While we've mentioned how stress can affect a guy's desire level, it can also give us a good run for our money when it comes to getting and keeping things up and running in the physical department too. It's common for most guys to experience erectile troubles now and then, especially now, related to all these new stressors that come with being a dad. New fathers often experience erectile problems, as well as low desire, due to a combination of factors: new changes in lifestyle that need to be nipped in the bud (not enough sleep, putting on extra weight, change in diet and exercise, starting to smoke, or to drink more than usual) as well as psychological issues, such as depression, anxiety, and a general feeling of being overwhelmed. Just because a guy has some erection problems now and then does not mean he has erectile dysfunction (ED). ED, which generally stems from physical causes such as heart disease, as well as age or an unhealthy lifestyle that might include being overweight, smoking, and drug use, is a more serious medical problem than the occasional mechanical malfunction.

> After the baby, for the first time in my life I had trouble getting it up—and keeping it up. I had been an avid runner, but the baby made me lose my routine and I admit I put on some pregnancy pounds right there with my wife. I was so stressed out and tired—nothing was working right.
>
> CARL, 34

PE makes us think of jumping jacks . . . but premature ejaculation (PE) brings to mind another kind of jacking. I often
hear from new fathers who, in the past, never suffered from
premature ejaculation, but now are suddenly finding themselves all too quick on the trigger. While it's easy to write it
off as a natural adjustment to getting back in the saddle and
suddenly finding yourself making love to a real woman as
opposed to your hand, I have another thought: It's the natural evolutionary response to a stressful situation, in this case
the possibility that a baby could wake up, or a child could
walk in. I've often said that premature ejaculation isn't a true
sexual disorder as much as it's just the way guys are wired—
not just for survival of the fittest, but for "survival of the
fastest."

According to Mark Jeffrey Noble, M.D., a consultant to
the Cleveland Clinic's Glickman Urological Institute, "One
might find some logical sense, from an evolutionary point of
view, to the idea that males who can ejaculate rapidly would
be more likely to succeed in fertilizing a female than those
males who require prolonged stimulation to reach climax."
So in that sense, maybe PE isn't a sexual dysfunction at
all—it's a completely normal way of functioning, based on
male physiology. If guys took hours to reach orgasm, we'd be
a much less numerous species. So not only is it healthy for a
guy to be able to ejaculate quickly, but think of all those
stressful sexual conditions primitive humankind had to deal
with: getting it on while worrying about wild animals and
warring tribes busting up the mood, or your head honcho

picking you as the next in line for a sacrifice to the gods. It's no wonder guys are wired to ejaculate quickly. We had to have some chance of propagating our DNA. So flash ahead to today's evolved metrosexual who's never had much of a problem holding off until suddenly there are all these new post-baby stressors in his immediate environment, and it makes sense that this evolutionary mechanism is being triggered. This is where turning off the baby monitor, putting a lock on the bedroom door, drinking a little wine before nookie time, even thinking about a low dose of an anti-anxiety medication might set things right and help us go from trigger-happy to, well, forgive the pun, a little more, shall we say, cocksure.

My main sexual problem used to be premature ejaculation. And even though it bothered my wife, she still thought of it as sort of a compliment. Since becoming a dad and getting both soft in the middle and over-anxious, now my main problem is not being able to get it up or keep it up. My wife takes it really personally. And she gets pissed off, especially when I finally get it up and then end up prematurely ejaculating. What's the point? No wonder half the time I'm not even interested in sex anymore.

HANK, 41

I've Got Desire Doldrums ... Maybe
I'm the One Who's Hormonal?

Is there really such a thing as "male menopause"? The conventional wisdom says that menopause is a "woman's condition," but as men advance into their forties they also experience a progressive decline in hormone levels, namely testosterone. The result can be andropause, which is estimated to affect about five million American men.

The hormonal decline that men experience isn't nearly as abrupt as it is in women—it's more like walking down a hill than jumping off a cliff. However, waning testosterone is likely to make a guy moody, irritable, and depressed. (Upon hearing this list of symptoms, one woman joked of her husband, "Is it possible he's had menopause since he was twenty?") A decrease in available testosterone also increases a man's risk for heart disease, and makes him more prone to injury because of decreasing bone density.

Andropause is not the same as a mid-life crisis, which is a psychosocial issue. And not all guys who experience aging, and the inevitable decline in testosterone that comes along with it, can be qualified as having andropause. Andropause is a medical condition, diagnosed with a blood test by a physician that reveals testosterone levels below a certain level. If a diagnosis of andropause is warranted, treatment with testosterone replacement may be an option, depending on a man's health history. Just as there are various hormone replacement therapies for women, there's also testosterone replacement therapy for men—and research is still ongoing into potential side effects.

However, the biggest, and most misunderstood, symptom of declining testosterone is a decrease in libido. Testosterone is truly the hormone that stokes the flames of desire. Many men confuse andropause with erectile dysfunction, because they often occur around the same time. These men often turn to an ED medication, such as Viagra, to improve their erectile ability, which works for a time in most cases. However, as men get older, the gap between desire and arousal widens and many men become deeply disappointed when an ED medication doesn't give them the desire to have sex. That's because it doesn't boost testosterone levels. The first issue for men, and their partners, is to accept the very concept of male menopause, talk about it as a couple, and, if they're concerned, make an appointment with an endocrinologist to check hormone levels. But beyond medical therapies, it's also about knowing, understanding, and accepting that sex evolves with the passage of life.

For guys who can embrace a deeper intimacy and open themselves up to a different experience of sex, the passage of time brings many rewards. Unfortunately, many men have a limited idea of sex, and they feel that if they're not having sex the way they were at age twenty or thirty, then something must be wrong! It's too bad more men aren't open and sharing of their experiences with each other, since changes in sexual function are so common. Fortunately, if women know what's going on and realize that hormonal decline can affect their partners, too, then they can take a proactive lead in starting a dialogue. For more on this subject, consider reading Jed Diamond's *Surviving Male Menopause: A Guide for Women and Men*.

I Might Have Postpartum Depression—Seriously!

Some of us guys live lives of quiet desperation and wait way too long before finally dealing with our issues. Many of the men I counsel are not just stuck in a rut, but also feeling generally blue. For new dads, is there a male equivalent of postpartum depression? There isn't much research into the subject, but in talking to other clinicians, I would say that rates of paternal depression range up to about 25 percent when there isn't concurrent PPD in the female partner and as high as 50 percent among men whose partners are experiencing postpartum depression. Rates are even higher in dads who work from home or stay at home, so it looks like there are a lot of sad SAHDs (Stay At Home Dads) out there. While men might not experience the hormonal changes that give rise to PPD, they do experience substantial life changes that can trigger depression.

What can you do? Help your guy find someone to talk to, starting with a professional. Also, help him get more guilt-free "guy time"—this won't bum you out as much now that you're doing more to take what you need, too. Right, moms?

It Might Be My Medication

As more and more guys take antidepressants such as Prozac, Zoloft, and Paxil to boost serotonin levels, they may reap a greater sense of calm or a more steady mood, but the price they may pay is decreased libido and delayed ejaculation. The combination often hits men like a double whammy: They feel inadequate that they can't reach orgasm, and then they worry about how they will explain it to a partner. They're "lustless on Lexapro" to put it plainly, or some other SSRI. Most people, and men especially, for better or worse, simply aren't comfortable discussing their depression with their partner. Still other guys may not even be aware that delayed orgasm and low libido are side effects of antidepressants. Ultimately, the key to great orgasms is good communication and, maybe, switching or balancing your medication if your doctor thinks it's appropriate.

Also:

1. *Consider a switch.* If you find that since going on an antidepressant your libido, your orgasm ability, or both have suffered, explore other options with your doctor. Wellbutrin may have a lower risk of sexual side effects.

2. *Make it, don't fake it.* When you're not feeling up for sex, tell your partner you want to cuddle or focus on her pleasure. Don't force yourself to have sex when you don't want to, and have it when you do.

3. *De-stress.* We all need to power down before we can get into the zone for sex. Start a new ritual of turning off the BlackBerry and the computer when you get home at night so you can tune into your partner.

4. *Discuss.* Tell your partner that you need to change up the

old bedroom routine if it's just not working for you anymore! Talk in terms of your fantasies and desires—not criticism. Sometimes, both people are harboring the desire for better sex, and it just takes one person to speak up.

5. *Easy does it*. You're not a porn star, so give yourself a break. Everyone goes through sexual ebbs and flows. Give yourself some time and try, as difficult as it may be, not to focus all of your energy on your orgasm.

I Need to Watch the Drinking Too (or Any Other Kind of Self-medicating, for That Matter)

Most of us know that having a drink or two before sex may help us relax and ease our inhibitions. But high levels of alcohol consumption can also result in sexual dysfunction. From causing the loss of erections to preventing your ability to get or stay aroused, alcohol disables the natural sexual response of the autonomic nervous system. But more than that, a lot of dads and moms use alcohol to self-medicate their way through the chaos of parenthood. Not to say there's anything necessarily wrong with that glass of wine or cocktail, but when alcohol (or any substance for that matter) becomes the main way of dealing with the natural disorder of parenthood, then it's potentially a problem. I dealt with this myself after the birth of my second son, when I started self-medicating my way through the (often endless-feeling) days. As an only child, I grew up in a quiet home. Nothing in my past had ever prepared me for the "wall of sound" that I'd encounter coming home to Owen and Beckett. Walking through the door, my life goes from calm to cacophony in an instant. Okay, sure, nothing beats getting greeted at the door with those jubilant little shouts of "Daddy!", but it didn't take long for the shouts to lead me to a shot or two of scotch. I'd never been a big drinker, and in fact I'd always made a point of not imbibing in light of a family history replete with alcohol problems. But after the birth of my second son, Beckett, it didn't take long for the wall of sound to wear me down. And I soon found myself savoring the difference between a smoky scotch from the Islay region versus a smoother single malt from the highlands. I knew things were getting bad when the holidays came and everyone bought me . . . well, take a guess.

So I talked to a therapist about my growing need to take the edge off by using alcohol, and he reassured me that over the years he'd worked with scores of new parents who found themselves extending the boundaries of cocktail hour and self-medicating their way through parenthood. From guys knocking back a six-pack a night, to *Deadwood*-style bourbon drinkers like myself, to mommies who like to lunch (and then some) over a bottle of white wine. So, where am I today? Dealing. I've chilled out on the drinking. Not completely, but more than partially. I've also started exercising before coming home whenever I can, which is really the dose of self-medication I need—iPod-enhanced, sweaty-palm-inducing, feel-good time on the treadmill. As of this writing, I'm thinner than ever, drinking less than ever, and dealing better than ever with the chaos of coming home. On a good day (which is most days), the wall of sound doesn't sound nearly so bad.

SEX RX FOR THE LADIES:
HEIDI'S MOST BASIC SELF-CARE TIPS

As you've probably figured out by this point, I refuse to do the "hot mom" thing. I really believe that shaving legs and getting a haircut, while they can help, are not the key ingredients to feeling sexy. That said, here are some of my basic self-care tips for moms:

- *Eat breakfast every day!* What mom said is true! It will kick-start your metabolism and keep you fueled. What you do diet-wise the rest of the day is between you and the food gods, but a good breakfast is a must. Also, if you need a snack during the day, treat yourself to trail mix. It's a jungle in here. Nuts for protein, chocolate chips for survival.

- *Drink water!* Seltzer water. Tap water. Water with lemon. Water with lime. Tea. You get the picture. While hydrating is good for all of us, this is doubly true if you're still nursing.

- *Exercise.* Walk ten minutes every day, with a stroller or strolling alone. The dog wants you. The dog needs you. Stretch a little every day to help appreciate your body. Try the "legs up the wall" stretch. Sit sideways on the floor beside a wall, knees bent, with one shoulder and hip touching the wall. Lower your back to the floor, with your legs bent, keeping your bottom close to the wall. Swing around to bring your legs up the wall, supporting yourself on your elbows and forearms. Lie there for a while, with your legs up the wall. Breathe. Be mindful of your body—not the one you want but the one you've got, right now. Feel the stretch, feel yourself relax. It feels surprisingly good. You can do this whenever you need a little break throughout the day.

- *Get dressed.* Yes, it can be depressing to put on clothes that don't fit anymore, but it's more depressing to find it's 6 p.m. and you're still in your sleep clothes. It's time to let go of the maternity wardrobe, give up on the skinny jeans, and go buy some clothes that fit you right now. It's well worth it.

- *Wear yoga pants and cool sneaks.* While sweatpants tend to say "I've given up," yoga pants tell the world, "Look at me—I've just come from yogalates!" (Right.) They also usually have a flattering cut for most bodies. The fact is, it's comfy to wear stretchy pants when you're postpartum and sneakers when you're running around all day. That's okay. But invest in some you really like.

- *Get a new bra.* Did you know that 85 percent of women wear the wrong size bra? If this wasn't true for you before, it probably is now. Now is the time to splurge on a proper fitting for your growing girls. Embrace them! It's amazing what a little "lift" can do for your body and your spirit!

- *And a bonus one to pass on to the guys*: This is awkward . . . but guys you should know that for some of us our sense of smell that was heightened during pregnancy is still going strong. This means it's on you to take extra care with your own hygiene. Brush, floss, scrub, rinse, deodorize, clean, wash, and primp all possible parts until our hearts are content. How will you know they're content? You'll ask! That saves us some awkward moments and potentially hurt feelings—like when we give you the cheek instead of the mouth.

SEX RX FOR THE GUYS: WORK YOUR LEAN MUSCLES ABOVE AND BELOW THE BELT

Hit the gym and pump some iron. There's truth to the phrase, "Use it or lose it." People who go without sex for extended periods often develop a "dearth of drive" and become habituated to living a sexless existence. In guys, testosterone levels go down, self-esteem plummets, and anxieties go up—so a little dry spell can quickly become a slump and lead to a vicious cycle. Studies have shown that single guys who work out and lift weights are more likely to have success with women and more sexual partners than guys who don't. It's not because women are more into brawn than brains, but because working out boosts testosterone as well as self-esteem, both essential parts of getting back in the game with gusto. If hitting the gym can help a single guy get his game back, the same holds true for Mr. Married with Children. In his book on male sexual health, *The Hardness*

Factor, Dr. Steven Lamm cites a British study in which men who reported having three or more orgasms per week experienced 50 percent fewer heart attacks and strokes as compared with those who had less frequent orgasms. According to Dr. Lamm, "On the surface, it looks as though the principal message of this study is that having sex reduces the incidence of heart attack and stroke and lets you live longer. In fact, just the opposite is true: being healthy allows you to have as much sex as you want."

SEX RX TO DO TOGETHER: LOOK AT ME, NOT THE TV

As we mentioned at the beginning of this chapter, couples who keep a TV in the bedroom have sex half as often as those who don't, according to psychologist Serenella Salomoni. Her team quizzed 523 Italian couples to discover how TV affected their love lives. On average, those who kept the TV out of their bedroom made love twice a week, or eight times a month. That dropped to four times a month for those with a television in the bedroom. So, get proactive—make one day a week a no TV day. Read books together on the couch, play cards, talk (what's that?!)—or better yet, get walking. You'll not only get in better shape physically, but you might be surprised what can get turned on when you turn off the big box.

IN CONCLUSION

While we hate to bid adieu with an '80s song thing again, and apologize in advance if you can't get this one out of your head, Olivia Newton John's exhortation to get physical and *let me hear your body talk* really does sum up this chapter better than we can. Bodies do talk—that's what sex is, right? Bodies talking, communicating, connecting on a deep level. If they're not happy and healthy bodies, that communication is going to get shut down or shut out. What's your body saying? That it wants to get "animal"? Or that it wants to eat animal? That it wants sweets? Or wants your sweetie? It's time to start listening to what we really need, not just food or rest, but living a really alive, sensual life. That doesn't mean you have to move to France and start rolling in lavender. It just means learning how to take a shower with your own full attention, appreciating your body for all it does for you, feeling the hot water as it hits your skin, the smell of the soap. It means taking a minute before scarfing down dinner to appreciate the food, where it comes from and how it really tastes going down. It means consciously making healthier choices in life and therefore love. So c'mon, put down the cookies and start working on getting some real sugar instead.

DIAGNOSE THIS!
YOUR LIBIDO LOWDOWN

As we've seen over the last couple of chapters, there's no one reason for libido loss, there are many: some physical, some mental, and sometimes it's that you married a clod. To help you find your very own libido lowdown, we've created the following quiz. Is it foolproof? Of course not. But you just might find out a little something about yourself or your partner that you didn't know before.

PART I: LEMME HEAR YOUR BODY TALK

1. My usual energy level is:
    A. like the Energizer Bunny
    B. pretty average
    C. a little below average
    D. slothlike

2. When it comes to shut-eye, I sleep:
    A. like a rock
    B. like a baby—5 to 6 hours or more at a time
    C. like my baby—3 to 4 hours at a time
    D. sleep? What's that?

3. I exercise:
    A. almost every day
    B. several times a week

C. maybe once or twice a week

D. when I get up to change the channel

4. Before kids, I thought about or had:

    A. lots of sex!

    B. sex

    C. a little sex

    D. not very much sex

5. My hormones are:

    A. my friends

    B. okay

    C. troublesome

    D. a bitch

6. When we do get together, sex with my partner:

    A. is body- and mind-blowing

    B. is good

    C. blows a little

    D. borders on necrophilia

Score!

For every A answer, give yourself 4 points

For every B answer, give yourself 3 points

For every C answer, give yourself 2 points

For every D answer, give yourself 1 point

If you scored 18–24, your body talk score is HIGHER

If you scored 13–17, your body talk score is MODERATE

If you scored 6–12, your body talk score is LOWER

PART II: BRAIN BAGGAGE

1. When it comes to sharing, I tell my partner:

    A. all my sweet nothings

    B. most things

    C. some things

    D. nothing

2. When I look in the mirror, I say to myself:

    A. boo-ya, baby!

    B. ya

    C. mostly boo

    D. Boo hoo!

3. This term best describes my life:

    A. strangely sane

    B. happily hectic

    C. bearably balanced

    D. multitasking mania

4. When I think about sex, I feel:

    A. sexy

    B. curious

    C. I don't

    D. bitter

5. Around the house, I get:

    A. lots of help

    B. some help

    C. occasional help

    D. treated like Cinderella

6. My mood is usually:

    A. happy happy joy joy

    B. pretty good

    C. up and down

    D. down and downer

Score:

For every A answer, give yourself 4 points

For every B answer, give yourself 3 points

For every C answer, give yourself 2 points

For every D answer, give yourself 1 point

If you got 18–24, your brain baggage score is LOWER

If you got 13–17, your brain baggage score is MODERATE

If you got 6–12, your brain baggage score is HIGHER

Key:

HIGHER BODY TALK AND LOWER BRAIN BAGGAGE:

Your brain and body appear to be in sexual harmony, both nicely on track. We're not sure why you bought this book! Maybe your problems are more logistical; you want to have sex, but you just can't seem to make it happen. Or maybe the sex you do have is dragging a bit or boring. Keep taking care of yourself physically and mentally, and check out chapters 5, 6, and 7 to figure out how to make date night work and put some spice in the sack. Look for the quickie in each moment, and recruit friends and family to take the kids out so you can stay in and have some fun.

HIGHER BODY TALK AND HIGHER BRAIN BAGGAGE:
Your body may say yay, but your mind is saying nay! Keep taking care of yourself physically, but now you need to pay special attention to your heart and mind. Time to weigh your emotional baggage: Clear the path to naughtiness with a good talk-sesh. Open up to your partner, a friend, or therapist about what's going on for you and how you to let it go.

HIGHER BODY TALK AND MODERATE BRAIN BAGGAGE:
Lookin' good! Your body says yay, but your mind says, sorta yay. Just work out some of those emotional kinks and you'll be on your way to kinky again. Clear the path to naughtiness with a good talk-sesh. Open up to your partner, a friend, or therapist about what's going on for you and how you to let it go.

MODERATE BODY TALK AND LOWER BRAIN BAGGAGE:
Lookin' good! Your brain appears to be on board but your body is not quite ready to back you up. You don't have to choose sleep over sex, you just have to figure out how to get

enough of both! Start with a physical checkup to rule out wacky hormones or other health problems. Line up some super sleep time, get regular exercise, and work on eating something besides leftover kid food.

MODERATE BODY TALK AND HIGHER BRAIN BAGGAGE:

Physically you may be dragging your heels a bit, but mentally you're headed for a screeching halt! While it might be good to see a doctor to pin down any physical problems, you most likely would benefit more from a head check. Are you burned out? Feeling undersupported? Hung up on sexuality for some reason?

MODERATE BODY TALK AND MODERATE BRAIN BAGGAGE:

Don't you just love being moderate? So safe and simple, right in the middle. Just "fine." But it's a slippery slope from "just fine" to "so-so" to "kinda sucky." Check out chapters 5, 6, and 7 to work on finding more passion in your life and see how your libido lights up.

LOWER BODY TALK AND LOWER BRAIN BAGGAGE:

The spirit is willing, but the flesh is as weak as Heidi's knees when she's deep in a good Johnny Depp fantasy. Your body is a temple, and yours needs a most honorable check in—let your doctor rule out any real problems and wacky hormones.

LOWER BODY TALK AND MODERATE BRAIN BAGGAGE:
While mentally you may be dragging your heels a wee bit, physically you're headed for a screeching halt! See above answer for getting physical with your physician and ditch extra brain baggage with a chummy chat. Line up some super sleep time, get regular exercise, and work on eating something besides leftover kid food. Remember, you don't have to choose sleep over sex, you just have to figure out how to get enough of both! Clear the path to naughtiness with a good talk-sesh. Open up to your partner, a friend, or therapist about what's going on for you and how you to let it go.

LOWER BODY TALK AND HIGHER BRAIN BAGGAGE:
Well, here we are, in the land of the lost libido. But you already knew that! If your partner is here too, then maybe the two of you can hole up in your nonsexual nest and take your own sweet time to figure things out. However, if you find yourself mismatched, miffed, and deep in Bickerland about the sexual state of things, there's only one thing to do: KEEP READING THIS BOOK.

CHAPTER FIVE

When Date Night Attacks: Why Long-term Love is So Dang Hard and How the Heck to Keep It Fun

LIGHTS, CAMERA . . . ACTION?

Here it is, date night. The thing that's going to save you from the excruciating sense of boredom you're feeling in your life lately, the thing that's going to bring you two back together, like you used to be. Never mind that you're not totally sold on the babysitter you managed to round up, or that it's raining cats and dogs, or that you have to be up early for an 8 a.m. division meeting. Never mind that you got no sleep last night because your four-year-old is still afraid of monsters and kicked and thrashed all night. Forget that Mom is downstairs freaking out because nothing in her closet fits. Forget you've been arguing all day about nothing. Forget that Dad is trying to get the kids to eat so they don't melt down later but melting down himself when he realizes that they're going to be 20 minutes late for their reservation and hence late for the theater. Forget that neither one of you really wants to go to dinner and theater. Forget that there are no cabs available. Never mind and forget it all. Empty your brain. Because it's date night. And !*&&*!!!%, you're going to have fun!

IAN: *Reading this, it makes me realize I am so over date night! The planning, the money, the pressure. Beyond that, what masochistic part of me continues to delude myself into thinking that we're actually people who are capable of committing to a plan? I give up.*

HEIDI: *But maybe that's what it's all about: giving up and then going out. It's like that Seinfeld episode where Jerry and George decide to create a show about nothing. Maybe we need to start not planning date nights. We need to go out and do nothing.*

IAN: *I like that. Go out with your sweetie and do nothing. Which is something that's actually pretty sweet.*

HEIDI: *Hey, while we're on the topic of scheduling time for love . . . what do you think of scheduled sex as a date night? Just committing to the act one night a week? I know it's not very romantic, and it lacks the spontaneity so many couples are already missing. But when is that mythical, spontaneous sex really going to happen? Who's going to tell the baby when it's a good time to nap?*

IAN: *Yeah, spontaneous sex is great when you can get it, but unfortunately, spontaneous sex is often the best sex you'll never have. You've got to be realistic. If couples don't make time for sex they might miss it altogether. Beyond that, as a sex therapist, I think there's really some virtue in just doing it and potentially jumpstarting the arousal. There's some truth to using it or losing it. Going through the motions can help you rediscover the motion, and remember that your sexual connection was what got you here into*

this whole mess in the first place. Trust that you can get back to that.
Try it, you'll like it.

HEIDI: *Totally. Sometimes it's not until JB and I are actually half-*
way through sex that I realize it's something I want.

IAN: *Sex begets sex; it's its own aphrodisiac. Sex raises testosterone*
levels and gets you interested in having even more sex. No wonder
then that couples in satisfying relationships tend to masturbate more
than couples with unsatisfying sex lives. Having sex eroticizes
you—body, mind, spirit.

HEIDI: *And remember—even if you have to schedule the time to*
hook up, you don't have to plan or schedule what happens during
that time . . . that's the fun part. That's the spontaneous part.

While date night has long been touted as a magic elixir for a
sickly sex and romance life, many of us know better. We know
how it is to be out—but wishing we were in. We know how it
can become just another chore, a wham-bam-thank-you-ma'am
of a dinner date or squeezed-in sex. We know how it feels when
you're out there and supposed to be having some special QT,
but instead you're just talking about your little cutie pies. And
we know all too well that strange sensation when we fight to try
to get back some of the fun of the "good old days" but all we can
hear is that Talking Heads song, asking us, "Well, how did I get
here?" How indeed? How did we go from hot and fun to snot
and runny noses? What happened to us? Where's the love,
man? Where's the excitement? No one told us marriage could
be so boring! And now with the kids . . . oy! "Same as it ever

was, same as it ever was. . . ." In reviewing a book on parental happiness by Arthur Brooks titled *Gross National Happiness*, says *The Economist*, "When researchers ask what parents enjoy, it turns out they prefer almost anything to looking after their children. Eating, shopping, cooking, praying, and watching television were all rated more pleasurable than watching the brats, even if they don't bite. As Brooks put it: 'There are many things in a parent's life that brings great joy. For example, spending time away from one's children.'"

Of course we all don't feel so strongly, and (of course!) our kids aren't brats (at least not yet, thank god), but we do need to take a good look at where we're having fun here. Really, the date night nightmare is a red herring, a symptom of a bigger issue: how to keep the fun and excitement alive, and how to fight the (unfortunate, not helpful) biology of long-term love. Here's the problem: Relationships come in three phases: *Lust, Romantic Love*, and *Attachment*. Now you may have to stretch your mind a bit to remember the *Lust* phase, or maybe— conversely—it's the only thing that you're thinking about these days. Lust is that can't-keep-your-hands-thoughts-or-other-body-parts-off-each-other time; in short, it's what got you into this whole mess in the first place. Good times. *Romantic Love* is the focusing of all that lust and the intense bonding that paves the way for the prolonged attachment phase of building and maintaining the nest. As many of us know, or at least hear, the romantic love phase is all too sweet and short, it's the phase we miss and lament, the thing we think about on dreary days, if/when we contemplate cheating, and the place that we often feel like we need to get back to, because really, it was pretty awesome. That leads us right here to the *Attachment* phase where you're reading a book together with a subtitle like *Getting It On Again*. You're attached, all right. At least in the "attachment parenting" sense, or maybe even at the hip, but certainly not at other crucial body parts.

So really, date night is a pretty good idea. It's based on the concept that relationships thrive on a sense of perpetual expansion (i.e., we keep growing as a couple). In the lust period, that sense of expansion happens naturally, when we stay up all night holding hands, fooling around, and getting to know everything (and everywhere!) there is to know about each other. But once we think we know everything about each other, our relationships stop expanding . . . and there's the rub. Er, lack of rub. And we're not just talking about in the bedroom. We're talking about in life. It is all too easy to get into a "comfortable" groove, especially when we're trying to give our kids well-deserved stability, that suddenly the newness/fun/novelty factors go *way* down. The idea behind date night is to bring those levels back up, to give the relationship a strong jolt to help sexy survive. We know date night is not as easy as it sounds. It's not as simple as getting new panties or scheduling sex. We know that, and we know you know that. But what we know that you might not know, however, is that it's the connections you make with your partner outside of the bedroom that lead back into the bed. It's an ongoing sense of fun, trust, playfulness, and emotional connection that naturally leads to expansion and excitement and physical connection.

What we're really talking about here are ways to make every day a little more like date night. We're talking about making a commitment to get intimate and emotional with each other and making time for sex. For a long-term relationship to win the biology battle, date night needs to become a life motto. Not on a grand chocolates and flowers scale, but on a little day-to-day, moment-to-moment scale. Novelty and newness in all your interactions and connections should become your mantra. Don't get us wrong: That could be dinner at some fabulous new restaurant you've both been dying to try, it could be a movie, it could be staying up late talking, or it could be sex in the back of the car if that's what floats your boat. But it should be a little piece of ass, er, fun, that reminds us our life is more than just a Talking Heads song—that we really do live a beautiful life, with another beautiful person.

CHEMISTRY 101

There's some basic brain chemistry happening when chemistry is happening. Neuroscientists, psychologists, and legions of other social scientists are actively trying to figure out the differences in the brain between "new love" and "old love" and if it's really possible to hold onto that feeling of romantic infatuation as a relationship goes on. Looking at our brains through the monitor of a four-ton FMRI—functional magnetic resonance imaging, really just a fancy photo-booth for the brain that registers chemical changes and blood flow—these neuroscientists can tell us a lot about what's going on chemically in there by measuring what happens while someone looks at a photograph of their beloved. In the case of new love, the scans reveal a lot of action in the part of the brain called the VTA (Ventral Tegmental Area). Which is also a hub for producing dopamine, the brain's natural stimulant and mechanism for feeling pleasure. No wonder newlyweds and others in the fresh throes of new mad love have VTAs that light up and dazzle.

Remember when you were head over heels in love and didn't care what anybody else thought, and found the fact that he uses baby-talk with his mother sort of cute and endearing? Well, it was dopamine activity helping you delude yourself. Once those levels wane, you take off the rose-tinted glasses and see him for the mama's boy he really is. So if you want to stay in it to win it, we have to find a way to put on those rose-tinted glasses again. As we ease into the long-term thing, our dopamine levels go down, and we've basically run out of Lite-Brite fun. The good news is that it's not a total blackout either. Something like date night, if done right, can be just the thing, adding some novelty, which automatically kicks in the dopamine transmission and gives us that little burst of energy and positive feeling.

DATE NIGHT: WHAT MOMS WANT DADS TO KNOW
Let's Let Go of Great Sexpectations

There's a difference between anticipation and expectation. Scheduling a regular time to have sex or looking forward to naughtiness on date night builds anticipation. Anticipation is excitedly licking your chops, stoking the flames of hope, looking forward with (hopefully) shared giddiness. Expectation is . . . just that. Something you expect, without thinking too much about it, without very much build up. Anticipation builds excitement, whereas expectation takes the fun out of it. Expectation can make sex on date night feel like a chore, where anticipation seems like something we can do together. And we like together.

Recently, when JB was gone on a business trip to California, I came up with this whole crazy night date plan. I fantasized that I would fly down to surprise him in his hotel room, have our older daughter spend the night at a friend's house, and leave the baby with my mom, who lives down there. I was super close to actually doing it, but got exhausted and blew it off, figuring instead I'd line up babysitting for when I picked him up and we'd be crazy and check into an airport hotel for a couple hours before coming home. But I couldn't find babysitting for the baby, so instead I came up with a new cockamamie plan in which I would time her nap just right and we'd still be able to check in somewhere and have some fun before she woke up. Right, what was I thinking? To make it all work, I frantically nursed the baby before

I left, so frantically, in fact, that I was late picking him up. When I finally got to the airport, instead of receiving a passionate kiss I was greeted with, "Gee, what took you so long?" And I exploded! Just like that, my whole fantasy was ruined! I was so far ahead of myself and so busy thinking about this grand scheme I couldn't deal with the real world. I was crushed and felt as if all my "work" planning things went to shit because he was an asshole and pointed out I was late. I think if I looked at this using a little of Ian's reORDERing technique again I can learn something about myself. Let's see:

- *Observe:* I was in manic planner mode, because I felt insecure about him being away and the fact we didn't have sex before he left.
- *Recognize:* Growing up in a chaotic hippie house, I never really knew what was going on or what to expect, who would leave or when they would come back. This left me feeling really vulnerable and insecure, and I dealt with it by using my imagination; I would plan and try to live every possible contingency in my mind so I could get used to it and I wouldn't be so surprised/let down/ freaked out when something went down. I still do this, I try to get control by worrying, or planning excessively instead of just living in the moment.
- *De-couple:* My mind was just getting the better of me. Learning to turn it off by taking a breath and feeling myself in my body helps me see things more clearly.

- *Engage* (in healthier behaviors): It would have been better if I just enjoyed the moment of seeing JB for what it was. We missed each other, it was sweet. Sure, we didn't rush to a motel and have crazy sex, but come on, we've got two young kids. And we did have good sex later that night once I calmed down and realized nothing bad was happening.

- *Regulate:* Next time I'll notice when I start to get carried away in my mind and try a little mindfulness to come back to "the now." It's not the first time I've hyped up expectations around date night or time alone. Date night is better in real life than in my imagination. I need to slow down and trust him more, and trusting in the moment and my ability to deal with whatever does come up. I can use my mindfulness techniques to work on this—I can also do this to get out of my head, and into my body, if we actually get around to having sex, too.

DATE NIGHT MINI RX: NOW YOU DO IT

Think of the last time your expectation got the better of you. Try reORDERing. Share this with your partner over dinner and call it a date.

Intimacy Rocks

Before we had kids my wife and I were constantly playing little pranks and practical jokes on each other—we were

**always striving for that "gotcha" moment. I really miss that
sense of fun and engagement.**

                                                                THOM, 27

Remember when we were engaged? Remember all that sex
that went with it? Here's a tip—the original definition of *engagement* means to challenge. Remember those days of challenging each other? When we worked to get each other worked
up? It's time to get back to that. A big part of what made you
so sexy to us then was the way you confided in us, the way
you opened up to us, the way we challenged each other to see
how smart and funny and sexy we could be. We felt as if we
were really getting to know you, and that you were seeing us
(and loving us) for who we really were. Those late-night talks,
early-morning confessions, and general sharing supplied us
with a powerhouse of intimacy that left us feeling electric.
Nowadays, when we only really see each other in passing, or
passing gas while we watch TV, we miss that sense of connection. When we don't connect during the day, we're not going
to want to "connect" at night.

DATE NIGHT MINI RX: NOW YOU DO IT

Intimacy is not a dirty word. Every single night, set aside
fifteen minutes to check in with each other about the
day. No TV, no distractions, no excuses.

Romance Is Rad

I love my husband, he is very supportive and is actually an excellent lover, but why is it he comes onto me with the same old lines? At the same time, a good-looking guy in the grocery store can get me all revved up when he flirts with me? THAT is driving me crazy. How can a perfect stranger cause such a strong reaction with just a look, or comment, and my husband can't? I want to feel beautiful, and sexy, and attractive. I want men to flirt with me, but I want all this from my husband, not a stranger.

MICHELE, 25

Oh how we miss those early days together where everything felt so darn good. The way we wooed each other, how we listened intently, how we couldn't get enough of each other ("You hang up first." "No, you hang up first." "No you." "Okay, we'll hang up together. . . .") It might have made our friends gag, but we liked it, a lot. Now you come home with Elmo balloons for the kid instead of flowers for us. Now we get caught up in poop schedules instead of scheduling time for us. And we don't like that so much. So here's the deal—it doesn't matter if you get us flowers we're allergic to, or chocolate we won't eat, or write us a poem you "borrowed" from somewhere. Maybe it's just watching us while we talk with a certain look that makes us stop and say, "What?" And you say, "You're just so beautiful, I still can't believe it." Or maybe it's as easy as renting a movie you know we like, even if it's not your favorite. It all works, because it reminds us of those early times, it makes us feel like we're special and loveable and the cream of your crop. Which makes us cream.

As JB and I come up on fifteen years of being together, we were recently talking about renewing our vows. At first this was just an elaborate excuse to go to Las Vegas and fuck like bunnies while the kids swim in the pool with Grandma, but the more we talk about it the more it makes sense. The things we would promise each other now are certainly different than those we made when we were ga-ga for each other all that time ago. We're thinking of it like this—the first time around our marriage was based on romance; we were hot for each other and that carried us through a lot of hard stuff. But this second one, well, it will be more like an arranged marriage. Hey, it works just fine for a good chunk of the world. It will be based on mutual interests, our families, financials, and so on. This way, we won't expect it to always be rosy. We won't expect to feel madly in love all the time. We'll have a grown-up kind of love this time, not the adolescent one we had when we were, well, adolescent. We know we will have to work to get to know each other, to see each other for who we really are, to keep learning about each other. We'll have to work for the sparks instead of thinking of them as a right. And then, when we're fucking like bunnies because we found some, it will be that much sweeter.

DATE NIGHT MINI RX: NOW YOU DO IT

Brainy date idea: Read *The Namesake* and have your own book club of two about it. Then rent the movie. Discuss. And/or make out. Not so brainy date idea: Rent the movie *Knocked Up*. Discuss. And/or make out.

Be My Playmate

Things are so dull. As Iggy Pop might sing: "No fun, my babe, no fun . . ." Where's the punk rock in life lately? What happened to the dangerous leather jacket of our young love? It's so easy for Mommy and Daddy to take over; to focus on the safe, the sterile, the grindstone of life. Work, kids, home, repeat. It's time to do something, as they like to say in preschool, "inappropriate." Let's go see music and grind together; let us feel the vibrations, the energy of the crowd, the explosiveness of a rowdy rock show. If mellow is more your style do the smoky, sultry jazz thing. Heck, maybe you're more metal—lighters up, dudes—we don't care. Just get us out there. Help us experience the sensuality of life. But this isn't (just) about the sex . . . it's about living a truly alive life that more easily leads to sex, that more easily leads to passion. Maybe it's skinny dipping, maybe it's wrestling on the beach, maybe it's going to a restaurant with a belly dancer instead of the usual steakhouse. Maybe it's spending the money you might have spent on an expensive dinner and theater on a motel room and for three hours make your own theater. The point is, you don't have to blow everything up to blow things off once in a while and cut loose. Do it to-

gether and remember the mantra: The family that plays together stays together.

DATE NIGHT MINI RX: NOW YOU DO IT

On your next arranged date, enjoy the Great Outdoors.
Have sex outside. Try not to get caught.

To Get It On, Get On It

This is another thing that often just falls on our womanly plates
by default. This can make us grumpy, and doesn't have a real
romantic touch. Surprise us and we might surprise you. Take
some initiative, don't count on us to make it happen. Think
proactive here. But it's not just planning logistics and setting up
the details, it's setting up the deal: Romance shouldn't be strictly
for date night, anticipation should be happening all the time.
Yes, do the legwork—hire that totally expensive sitter, buy tickets to a play, line up a playdate. But then, get on to the real work
of wooing. Romance is a day-to-day thing, it takes real effort,
halfheartedly doing it, or forgetting about it makes us feel like
we're halfhearted about us . . . which doesn't make us cream.

DATE NIGHT MINI RX: NOW YOU DO IT

Have the nonplanner of you two plan the next entire
date night, including tracking down child care and making sure everyone is happy and fed before leaving. What
was different about the date? Better? Worse? Stay up
after you get back and give appropriate (or inappropriate, if you're naughty like that) feedback.

And While You're At It

Keep this in mind . . . one of the biggest hurdles of date night is often the night part! Nighttime is not always the right time. Night is hard for parents—exhausting days at work and with kids, hormone levels low, food intake at minimum, crankiness at premium. Try setting the clock half an hour early and having an early-morning breakfast date, when everything just seems brighter. Better yet—take a day off and stay in bed. Play hooky, have morning mimosas, and see where the day takes you.

> We finally kicked the kids out of the bed. I had forgotten how nice it was to go to bed naked with my husband. Things happen so much easier when the opportunity is there.
>
> SHAWN, 40

> Sex has become kind of naughty again . . . we have to sneak around, hoping not to wake someone up or get caught and have to explain that to a two-year-old! It adds to the fun—like being in high school again.
>
> AARON, 26

DATE NIGHT MINI RX: NOW YOU DO IT

Date night? Forgettaboutit! Call in sick or late, pawn off the kid, and take a date day instead.

I Need Date Night—With Myself

We love our BFFs, and girl's night is always a big hit. However, sometimes the best date night is the date night we have alone. Meaning not with you or anyone else. The same things that make us great at being moms make it hard for us to be who we really are. Sometimes what we need is time to figure out who we are outside of us as a couple. Then we can bring that new knowledge back into our relationship and we'll both remember there's a lot more to us than just the day-to-day selves. How do we find that time? You offer to watch the kids, buy a book you think we'll like, remind us of a hobby long forgotten. JB was awesome about getting me to play soccer again, something he knew I used to love. He passed my name on to a friend who was starting a team, and never complains when I come home at 11 p.m. from a late game. And he's reaped the rewards—not only is exercise is an aphrodisiac (and so is a night away from baby, bumping into sweating guys), but I like him to kiss my bruises and bumps. I like to show him just him just how much fun I had by having more with him. Whether it's soccer, knitting night, or just a long bath and some solo time, encouragement like this works across the board. Because happy, healthy, whole women like sex more. It's that simple.

DATE NIGHT MINI RX: NOW YOU DO IT

Hang date night up to dry. Spend time instead with friends or yourself. Go for it: one babysitter, two separate date nights.

DATE NIGHT: WHAT DADS WANT MOMS TO KNOW
Date Night Sucks

Getting out with you once every two years (I mean two weeks) should be a fun evening of escape from it all, but all too often it ends up feeling like more of the same. Why is it that date night always seems to be a choice between sitting across from each other at a restaurant and secretly panicking because we have nothing to say to each other, hanging out with another couple from our kids' school, and, surprise, talking about our kids, or doing something that feels exhausting and taxing? (Why oh why did we buy those theater tickets four months ago?)

From the anxiety of having to spend five hundred bucks just to go out to dinner with that couple who likes to yammer on about their trips to Canyon Ranch and order way too many bottles of expensive wine, to worrying about getting home before we have to pay the sitter for another hour, to listening to you worry about how the kids are doing with the sitter, date night can be a real downer. Hanging out with other parents or doing the same old thing shouldn't even count as a date night. Date night at heart should take us away from our role as parents, it shouldn't involve other people who remind us that we're parents, it shouldn't hold a mirror up to life—it should allow us to escape from it. We need to talk about something other than the kids, to shed this mom and pop skin for a little while, to escape into some other sides of ourselves.

DATE NIGHT MINI RX: NOW YOU DO IT

Find a quiet place to sit together, grab something to drink, and find out what Dad thinks a perfect date would be. Just listen.

I Need a Date Night with the Guys Sometimes

Man, I miss just hanging out with the guys—as much as I want to go out with my wife, I really also want a night away from her.

DON, 29

Okay, now that we've told you how we really feel about date night, it's time for you to know something else. Even though you're our best friend, the mother of our children, and the love of our lives, this Friday night we'd really like hang out with our buddies and catch that re-run of *Star Trek 2: The Wrath of Khan*, complete with commentary from Ricardo Montalban. Please don't make us feel even more guilty (or, okay, dorky) about it. We know we never get to go out and do stuff together; we know that we constantly complain about how we just want to spend quality time together (i.e., have sex); and we know we promised you a night at the ballet. But here's the thing: As much as we love you, you're, well, not a guy. And now that we're dads, what we need is to blow off some steam with our buddies, get away from it all for just a few hours and come back recharged and rejuvenated.

DATE NIGHT MINI RX: NOW YOU DO IT

All right. *Wrath of Khan* it is . . .

Let's Maybe Not Spend the Whole Night Sitting Across From Each Other Gazing into Each Other's Eyes

Anthropologists have long observed that women are face-to-face communicators, while men do so side by side. This means that women are much more comfortable with direct eye contact, which probably has a lot to do with the female history of nursing, cuddling, and generally fawning over their infants all the while staring lovingly into those big baby eyes. Men, on the other hand, find direct eye contact extremely confrontational. As Helen Fisher wrote in her remarkable book, *Why We Love*, "This response probably stems from men's ancestry. For many millennia men faced their enemies; they sat or walked by side as they hunted game with their friends." No, I'm not saying we should sit around a fire and cut up a yak carcass, but if your idea of date night involves staring into each other's eyes with nothing but a $90 bottle of wine between us, it could lead to more tension and confrontation than soothing conversation. Let's pick activities that allow us to do things together that don't depend on lots of talk, but get us out there doing something. And remember, just because we don't want to talk endlessly about "us" doesn't mean we don't love "us." We just might show it differently, like by grilling you meat, for instance.

DATE NIGHT MINI RX: NOW YOU DO IT

Throw the kids in strollers and head out for a walk, play a board game instead of watching TV together, trade fifteen-minute massages. The point is to just do something together.

Adrenaline Makes My Heart Grow Fonder

We had three hours in our house without kids and my wife wants to rent a movie.

GREGG, 39

Hey, let's do something fun for once. And I don't mean going to the PTA meeting or talking endlessly about "our relationship." I mean different! Put the baby down, and let's just go! For some fathers, one of the hardest things to deal with is the sense of routine that comes along with parenthood. Once, we were young and free, without a care in the world. (Are you done rolling your eyes?) Now everything is scheduled, planned to the nth degree, and endlessly repeated to the point that even date night starts to feel predictable and pressured. It's great that we're so comfy together, but I need to get fired up. So let's break out of the usual and go for the gold now and then. Long-term relationships are based on trust, predictability, responsibility, and dependability, but sexual attraction is based on mystery, danger, and unpredictability. To get some of that lust back, we don't have to give up that attachment, but we have to look outside of it (if just for an evening) for something to get our hearts racing again—so we can start rocking each other again.

> I'm thinking, how am I supposed to last another 40 years with this guy? Where's the excitement?
>
> TRACY, 44

> Somewhere in the last five years we've forgotten how to French kiss...
>
> TOM, 30

DATE NIGHT MINI RX: NOW YOU DO IT

It can be hard to really explore naughtiness when the kids can rat you out at any time. If you can't get it together to actually be naughty, read naughty stories to each other. Find ones you like, and share why.

Let's Make Romance Rad Again

Forget everything you were ever told about romance—let's not spread rose petals on the sheets, but go get it on in the neighbor's garden. Okay, maybe everything doesn't have to come down to a little danger, but I do think we live in a culture where romance has become a Valentine's Day cliché, and eclipses so many other aspects of what it means to be in a dynamic charged sexual relationship. The flowers, the chocolate, and so on become shorthand to avoid really communicating. But maybe I've had too much time to think about it and am just too self-absorbed to see, or really admit, that a little romance goes a long way. Maybe there really is a place for some good old-fashioned romance.

I guess the big word here is *communicating*. I mean really communicating, not saying cheesy lines because "we're supposed to," but being honest, and open, and loving with each other.

DATE NIGHT MINI RX: NOW YOU DO IT

Share the most romantic memories you have of each other. What's most surprising? Most touching? Now, touch.

Not Everything Has to End with Sex

Too many times we set up date night as "sex night"—only to have it come off half-cocked . . . sorry. And too often I come home from date night with a bloated stomach and migraine (about to get worse once I write a check to the babysitter) and know if I don't have sex, or if I don't at least make an effort to want to have sex, that Lisa will be insulted, and the night will go down as another date-night disaster. The truth is there are so many times us guys want to have sex with you, so many times we think sexy thoughts from our mental libraries of sexy experiences, and all we want to do is crawl under the covers with you, have raunchy sex, and then go make nachos and eat them in bed. But it's often not post–date night. Let's agree to disentangle sex and date night. If date night ends up feeling like a chore, so too is the sex that often follows. Since we've agreed on the fundamental principle that date night (or date day) should be unpredictable, let's not commit to sex being a done deal. Like a genuine bonafide first date, let's see where things go.

Some of our best date nights happen on the fly; we watch a silly movie together after the kids are asleep, or we stay up late and instead of working, sit together on the stoop in the dark drinking wine, talking. It doesn't lead to sex usually, which may be why it's so successful, but it's like foreplay for the next week. It's the idea that he wants to hear what I have to say, that he thinks I'm interesting or that we have something to talk about. When we're doing something together like that I don't have to worry about how to make sex work, how to fit it in. And amazingly, that's when it ends up happening, that's when we end up with the spontaneous stuff.

JEANNIE, 33

DATE NIGHT MINI RX: NOW YOU DO IT

Fool around but agree there will be no sex. No matter what! Touch, caress, play, but NO sex allowed. What do you do instead? Where do things go with that off the table? No cheating!

The truth is that we pretty much never have sex on weeknights anymore. I am just way too tired and frankly would prefer to de-stress with a bath or cheesy TV show. So instead we plan weekend sex; when the baby is out on a playdate with Grandma, we have our own playdate.

T. D., 35

SEX RX FOR THE LADIES:
HAS YOUR LOVE NEST BECOME MORE LIKE A BIRD'S NEST—FOR THE WHOLE FLOCK?

Take some time create a love nest. Get rid of the baby gear, buy some new sheets that aren't peed on or puked on. Choose fabrics that feel good, colors that relax, and smells that make you think of something other than baby. Make a grown-up get away space that appeals to all your senses, so you can maximize the time you do have—a little sexy, sensually stimulating and relaxing haven to escape to after the kids are down or while they're with the sitter. Make it a place to leave your day-to-day roles behind.

HEIDI: *That said, it doesn't have to be the bedroom. Maybe you're not ready to kick the kids out . . . I have to admit I like it when they're in bed with us. I like waking up to kid breath or a half-pint foot in the face. It's sweet—not to mention half the time JB's out snoring on the couch anyway. Many of us are co-sleepers; either because we planned it that way or it's just how it ends up every night.*

IAN: *Yeah. And can we all just admit that yes there have been times when we've had sex with a sleeping baby in bed with us. Sure, it's not our first choice, and yeah, it limits the potential for acrobatics, and yes, we have to be very very quiet, but having a baby in our bed does not necessarily mean we're not having sex.*

HEIDI: *Right on. But be responsible—build a wall of pillows or something. For me it has to be out of sight, out of mind.*

SEX RX FOR THE GUYS: FREE TO BE . . . ME AND ME

Buddy time is good, but make sure you also give yourselves a chance to tune out the external noise and tune in to your internal voice—and not the voice that's anxious and worried. Go ahead and introduce yourself. A friend of Ian's is really into anthropological archetypes and has spent a good part of his life thinking about and cultivating these different types within himself. When he talks about the Hero part of himself he doesn't mean someone endowed with superhuman powers, but a person in the real world who keeps things moving forward and gets the job done. It got us thinking that many of the parents we know are heroes every day—getting the job done. But it also got us wondering if maybe, as parents, we get stuck in this hero role and forget to access other parts of ourselves. Maybe as a couple it's time to do something completely totally new that pushes us back into innocence. Or maybe we do need to be a group member and go out and do something with a bunch of people, but not the same old groups that we meet out of obligation or familiarity. Maybe there's a seeker inside of you that longs for something deeper, more connected, dare I say spiritual. Or maybe there's an inner artist that's been evicted from your heroic life. Or a joker that yearns to laugh again, or play a prank, or do something naughty, devilish, and very un-heroic. Think about some of the different types that reside within you, aspects that you used to put more effort into embracing, or always wanted to, and try to translate them into date nights.

TO DO TOGETHER: DATE THERAPY

Did we mention that couples therapy is a date night? Seriously, schedule an appointment with a therapist and use it as a chance to talk, reflect, and learn more about each other. We're not talking sex therapy either, which tends to be narrow and often problem-solving oriented, but good old-fashioned talk therapy. When the therapist asks why you're coming to see him or her, don't think about the problems you want to discuss, but rather your hopes and aspirations.

If I May Chime In: Heidi

And sometimes you have to keep trying until you find a therapist you both like. We finally did, and it worked wonders for our love life. We'd go in all pissed off, betting each time on who was in the right, who was going to "win." Each time, though, she managed to make us feel like we each had won. She helped us see what was really going on underneath the Bitch and the Asshole. And there's something about the way she brought out JB's emotions that transferred directly to the bedroom. I just can't help myself when he starts to get all teary and husky-voiced. Emotions are hot—what can a girl do?

IN CONCLUSION

Your life doesn't need to turn into a scene from Night of the Living Date. Ideally, date night is happening all the time, in little pieces here and there, showing interests and appreciations, and supporting grown-up lives and grown-up needs. While this chapter is focused on date night, really we're talking about how to make every day a date day—and it has to do with staying connected. This really contributes to lasting sexual desire and fulfilling sexual experiences. For example: nonsexual physical intimacy, such as hugging and holding hands, laughing together, or playing little pranks on each other, leaning into each other while you watch television, cleaning up together after a meal, sharing the day's events and genuinely listening, and so on. While these interactions and connections may not seem inherently sexual, they help to generate a reservoir of transferable desire and a greater disposition toward sexual desire.

So go ahead and drop the great sexpectations and date night version one. Instead, be spontaneous. Go on a date day: Call in sick, drop the kids off at school, and go have lunch and a couple of glasses of wine and fun back at home. Engage in silly public displays of affection. Go to a 1 p.m. movie where there's nobody else in the audience. If date day isn't in the cards, then stick with date night, but don't plan anything—just get out and go wherever the night takes you. Making date night work is like being a detective tracking down a wily suspect—we need motive and opportunity (let's face it, means is not an issue, our kids are evidence of that), but mostly we have motive: none. And opportunity: not knocking. Date night is really just about the hard work of being a good gumshoe—putting opportunity in the spotlight again and building a strong case of motive-ation. With any luck you'll be hard (!) boiled in no time!

DIAGNOSE THIS!
INSPIRE MORE DESIRE

To what degree does your relationship have a reserve of transferable desire, or to what extent are you stuck in a "nontransferable" relationship? Is it rare for you and your partner to have any sort of nonsexual physical intimacy? Are you living under the same roof but in different worlds? Take a few minutes to think about this, and write down anything that comes to mind. Consider the following activities. How often do you engage in them on a weekly basis? Would your partner be likely to respond in the same way?

1. Hug/embrace
2. Hold hands
3. Kiss
4. Say "I love you"
5. Call during the day to say hi and check in
6. Compliment each other
7. Email each other

8. Eat meals together
9. Take time to really talk about each other's day
10. Do chores together
11. Go on date nights regularly
12. Watch favorite TV shows or read the newspaper together
13. Socialize with others together
14. Cultivate/participate in mutual hobbies and common interests
15. Go on vacations together

If you engage in at least twelve of these activities four times a week or more, you're definitely connected on an emotional level. If not, try to think about ways to increase the frequency of positive interactions in your daily life. You'll be surprised how easy it is once you get started.

Now consider some of these other activities, which are more directly linked to desire. On a weekly basis, how often do you do the following?

1. Kiss tenderly
2. Fool around without the expectation of immediate sex
3. Compliment/comment on each other's sexual attractiveness/sexiness
4. Call each other up during the day and flirt
5. Talk about sex/fantasies

6. Engage a sexual sense of humor/get bawdy with each other
7. Dress provocatively for each other's eyes only
8. Engage in playful exhibitionism
9. Engage sexually outside of the bedroom
10. Read erotic literature/watch erotic films together

If you engage in half of these activities or more at least once a week, you are still sexually connected and erotically charged. If not? Well, then, you're just like the vast majority of couples in long-term committed relationships. You might be happily committed, but you're in a sexual rut! Then again, chances are you knew that already or you wouldn't be reading this book.

So how do you get out of this rut? Try to integrate some of those activities into daily life.

If it feels awkward or out of character—which is fairly likely—do it on your own terms.

You don't have to parade around in a bra and g-string for your partner, or bulk up your biceps. If talking sexy on the phone seems a bit stilted, try a slightly naughty email instead. Be creative. Do what is comfortable, but think about ways to modify the above lists so that you can build at least one of these general suggestions into your daily routine.

CHAPTER SIX

Naughtiness Is Not Just for Kids: How to Spice Up Sex So You Actually Want It

LIGHTS, CAMERA . . . ACTION?

Picture this: The lights are off. The room is dark. Two bodies come together: not out of raw passion, but more out of conjugal duty. The action unfolds briskly and efficiently; hands move adeptly and knowingly over bodies, and without even breaking a sweat the tension swells, appears to peak, then subsides, with nary a pant. Requisite tokens of affection are given and received. Expedited cuddles, affirmations of love exhaled like remnant vapors, and a synchronous turning away to their respective sides of the bed. Another night of sexual détente. But better this fragile concord than an admission of the truth Mom thinks to herself: Yet another orgasm has been faked in the name of sex-after-baby peace. Little does she realize that over on the other side of the mattress, Dad is thinking the very same thing. Nope, it's not a marriage on the rocks, not a villianous war on love. It's something far more insidious . . . it's Tuesday. Night. Sex.

HEIDI: *Whoa! Yikes, wait. Guys fake it too? Who knew?*

IAN: *Sure. We're all familiar with the now-infamous orgasm scene in* When Harry Met Sally. *Meg Ryan is sitting across the table from Billy Crystal and launches into a full-blown orgasmic performance to demonstrate over corned beef and rye that, yes, women fake orgasm and men often have no idea. But men fake it too, often for the same reasons that women do—a sense of pressure, too much stress or an inability to communicate about things that might be bothering him, whether in bed or in his relationship.*

HEIDI: *Hey, I know that trick . . .*

IAN: *Granted, it may be a little trickier for guys to pull off convincingly, but it's not so hard: Tense up your body, thrust and pant, and spasm.*

HEIDI: *Gee, Ian, you're so romantic.*

Okay, so here you are: the big bedroom chapter. The good news is you've made it this far; you're working things out, you're building anticipation, you're working on getting more spice into your life outside the bedroom. Now it's time to start doing it in the bedroom. Do we hear a deep sigh? What if the cold hard truth of the matter is that the real reason you're not getting it on is because sex is . . . well, boring. Maybe sex has always been sort of boring for you, maybe you've never been comfortable saying what really turns you on, or been able to let go and relax into it. Or maybe you used to have great mind-blowing sex, and now it just blows. Either way, here you are. And if you're looking for an excuse to NOT change things, parenthood is full of 'em. While it's great to be super-comfortable with each other ("You forgot to flush again . . . !"), sometimes this closeness and our new roles as co-parents can keep us from taking a childlike approach to ourselves and our sex lives, one where we are creative, can let go easily and use our imagination. This is probably due to the fact that there are two types of sexual arousal: psychogenic and physical. Psychogenic is basically just a fancy way of saying that we can get turned on without ever having to have any physical contact. This is what we had in yonder past, this is desire: Sexual anticipation actually giving us a physical sense of aching, our minds were leading our bodies.

But sexual arousal is also stimulated physically. Maybe it starts with a kiss, but it quickly leads to a lot of genital friction and getting off. So sometimes you just got to get in there and jump-start things. The problem is that it's easy for strictly physical sexual arousal to become sort of like changing a diaper: something we do with a sense of know-how, efficiency, and routine, and lots of little shortcuts that have become automatic. This is what we've got to beware of; this is where fun and fantasy can keep us from strictly getting off to thinking off, to re-engaging our minds and reinvigorating a lackluster love life. You may know each other's bodies more intimately and be able to provide each other with more dependable, frequent, even more intense orgasms, but, still, the spontaneity and sense of surprise have diminished over time. It's time to dig deep and uncover a new love map together.

This "love map," a term first coined in 1980 by Dr. John Money of Johns Hopkins University, refers to "the sexual template expressed in every individual's erotic fantasies and practices." The more we make our love map out together, the more fun we can have, and now more than ever you know we need that. The surprising thing, however, is that parenthood is also full of new sexual opportunities. It's a chance for us to switch things around, to take "boring comfort" and turn it into open trust. It's a chance to take stability and turn it into a safe playground. With a little creativity and a lot of communication, in no time we can get back to what we had before and more . . . we can get sex that's actually worth having; we can become best friends with FULL benefits.

"Given the mediocre sex that lies behind common complaints of sexual boredom, low sexual desire often actually reflects good judgment. Rather than focusing on the low-desire partner, clinicians should wonder more about the high-desire partner who often wants more of the usual—often he or she does not know enough about sex or intimacy to realize the sex he or she is having may not be worth wanting."

DR. DAVID SCHNARCH,
THE PASSIONATE MARRIAGE

NAUGHTINESS: WHAT MOMS WANT DADS TO KNOW
Don't Call Me Mommy

The baby seems so pure—I just don't want to do anything "dirty" these days.

KRISTIN, 26

Motherhood came as a surprise to me, and although I love it deeply, I now see only glimpses of who I was before my son was born.

AMY, 43

In Chapter 3 we talked about the importance of turning a woman's brain off to turn her on. That's just one more good reason to help us leave our mommy personas at the bedroom door. Especially since society has such a weird mother/whore thing going on, we've already got lots of mixed messages about what it means to be a mom—what good girls or good mothers do and don't, and how to balance that with who we really are. For some of us, mommy and sex need to be separated like church and state. We just can't get into it if there are baby toys around or you've hit on us while playing peekaboo. We need to be free to be our naughty selves, and define our own versions of what good mommies do. So please, please don't call us "Mommy"—unless we are actually your mother, and you're a toddler, and you're reading this, which would be pretty weird. Instead, call us "sweetie" or "lover" or "sexy lady." Talk grown-up with us, take us grown-up places, buy us some grown-up lingerie. But don't. Ever. Call us. "Mommy."

Or Any Other Family Member for That Matter . . .

Does familiarity breed more than just contempt, but boredom as well? Perhaps. Let's get biological for a minute, here. The boredom that often accompanies sexual familiarity is a function of what's known as the Westermarck Effect, or reverse sexual imprinting. Sexual imprinting is the process by which a young animal learns the characteristics of a desirable mate. Reverse sexual imprinting occurs, however, when two people live in domestic proximity during the first few years of life, like a brother and sister, and become sexually desensitized to each other. From a Darwinist standpoint, reverse sexual imprinting serves a valuable natural function, as an instinctual mechanism for avoiding the genetic problems that can result from incest. Yay biology! Good call. But could the Westermarck Effect occur in relationships between lovers as well? Does the deep-seated taboo against familiarity make sex less sexy? Boo! It doesn't have to be so. Break free of the Westermarck Effect and make your own. Get resensitized to each other. Try this: Put your hand right over your partner's body, as close as you can without touching. Feel their energy and experience your own. Try to find something new about their body you've never noticed before. (I would add that discovering leftover baby fat and pointing it out might send you right back to the Westermarck and beyond! Find something else!)

Naughty Is Nice

So keep an open mind, and don't make us feel ashamed to show our naughty sides. If we want to try something new, or bring things up a notch, support that. As I mentioned above, some of us really struggle with letting go of being "good girls"—especially "good mothers." The more you can coax and encourage us into breaking out of that, the better. One of my naughtiest nights with JB happened quite by accident. We were in a hotel room on vacation and I took extra time getting myself dressed in the little dressing room, putting on stockings and sexy things I don't usually wear. JB was waiting in the bedroom, and I liked that we were separate while getting ready. I liked it so much I thought that it would be fun to sneak out the door and knock, and present myself to him. So once dressed, I yelled I was getting a soda, went to the hallway, took some breaths, and knocked on the door. When he opened it, thinking I was locked out, he sized me up in such a way that before I knew it I was saying, "Are you the guy who called for a date?" I was so embarrassed to say that at first—I thought he might be confused, or bust out laughing, or even make fun of me. But he instantly went with it, opening the door for me with, "So, what's your name?" It was so cheesy, so awkward at first and different from anything we had done. But it was also really hot. From that point on it got easier and easier as we got more and more lost in role-playing and fantasy. Each time one of us took a chance by taking it further, or staying in character, or being sweet and flexible, we really were standing up for our future sex life. Yes, it was a little painful at first, but we rode it out and then we rode each other, for a long time, happily, in the sacred space we created in that room that night.

Quality, Honey, Not Quantity

At one point my husband asked how the sex was and I was like, "Oh, orgasm shmorgasm, who cares"—and I knew we were in trouble.

                                                    PETRA, 32

Good sex matters. Good sex gives us something yummy to look back on during our busy days. One of the biggest mental shifts you can make to encourage sexy is to stop thinking in terms of quantity and start thinking in terms of quality. For lots of women, it takes a lot more work than just the ol' in out in out to make sex gratifying. It takes some investment and time, which as we know is in high demand lately. For this reason, many of us would rather have one great mind-blowing night of sex twice a month than have so-so sex a couple nights a week. It gives us something to think back on and get excited about. There are some sexual encounters JB and I have had that as soon as I remember, I still get a little wet. Then there are others. . . . It's not because JB was bad in bed those times, but rather because we rushed, we forced it, I wasn't fully present, or something else got in the way of a real connection. For me, the better sex is, the more I remember how I like it. And it's remembering that that pushes me to make more space for it in my life. So really, quality breeds quantity. And then everybody wins.

That Said . . . Think Fast

Okay, yes; good, long, patient, yummy sex is better. But let's be realistic. How much time do we really have here? We're dealing with a million variables. And sometimes, like you guys, we just want to fuck or get fucked. It doesn't have to be a big fireworks thing. We might not shoot buckets, but it's still hot, it still turns us on and makes us excited and gives us something to look back on. When we have a little quickie, or even think about the little quickie we'd like to have, it inspires us to get down to the basic "units" of what turns us on and what doesn't. Little quickies are a great way to get our adrenaline going, as well as explore and get acquainted with our own unique love maps, something that is hard for busy parents to really get down and dirty with. From hand jobs to frisky playful exhibitionism to just taking a moment to feel each other up, quickies are a way of re-connecting and building up a reserve of sexual anticipation. While not supersatisfying, there is a time place for them. Taking the big O out as a "goal" really leaves more room for playful, fun stuff—as long as we know we can get that other fulfillment later. We might also add that quickies are a pretty darn fun way of taking a break from the grind of parenting chores.

FAST-FOOD FOR THOUGHT:
HEIDI AND IAN'S FAVE McQUICKIES

HEIDI:

- Saturday morning cartoons downstairs, Saturday morning copulation upstairs.
- JB always likes out-and-about naughtiness. This was easier when we found ourselves at degenerate house parties at the end of a date, rather than downtown after eating at a nice restaurant with a babysitter waiting at home. Most recently, after using half a tank of gas in search of a semi-private spot we ended up on some deserted ghost property downtown that looked like where The Hulk came to life. We were jittery but determined, that is until the cops drove by and the babysitter, aka my dad, called to see when we'd be home. Needless to say, it didn't happen that night, but the excitement stayed with us for a week until we could once again take advantage of Saturday morning cartoons.
- Riding JB (facing him) while he sits on potty (seat down, of course!). This is especially fun for me since my first orgasm ever happened this way in the bathroom of my boyfriend's parents' house. Memories . . .
- "Saving water" by showering together. Makes all kinds of giving and/or receiving fun and oh so clean! No wonder our bathroom is the only room with a working lock!

IAN:

- I agree with JB about out-and-about naughtiness, or what I call playful exhibitionism—the thrill of getting caught/seen/watched provides an extra jump-start of excitement.
- Catching Lisa in those quick moments of undress when she didn't know I was lurking about or looking at her.
- Hopping into the shower and getting shampoo in her eyes.
- Sleeping over at someone else's house: I guess that ties into the out and about playful exhibitionism.

Replace the Batteries in My Vibrator, Don't Get Jealous of It!

A vibrator is a great way to compromise between the slow sex many of us women need and the speedy sex our busy lives allow. These trusty gadgets can turn an otherwise fruitless bite-size quickie into a satisfying high-protein smoothie! In just minutes! Beyond that, vibrators and other toys help us explore our own sexuality for ourselves . . . not for anyone else. C'mon—you know we need some alone time when our favorite vibrating "toy" is a bouncy seat. Don't worry, guys, just because we want to play with ourselves doesn't say anything about you. It just means we're committed to the cause, and sometimes, it's simply quicker, easier, cleaner, and less complicated to take care of ourselves.

I used to feel like a vibrator was my competitor. Now, as a stressed-out dad, "the purple gizmo" is my best friend.

SEAN, 31

Sometimes We Fake It ... Sometimes We Fake It to Make It

I made a pact with myself to just do it. I made a bed on our living room floor, lit some candles, and actually got naked! I even quickly forgave him for not putting on music, or partici-pating in setting the mood.

JULIE, 32

As we said before—sometimes we fake it because we feel obligated to give you sex, because we want to cross it off our list, because we're worried about our relationship. But there are other reasons too, more ambiguous ones, such as that we love you and want to make you happy. While we may not necessarily want sex, we sure just want to have had sex so we can float around with that good feeling—no, not orgasm, the other one—that everything is all right and good be-tween us. And then sometimes we fake it to try to make it; we're hoping it might spark some real feeling in us. When we were all young and in love and full of hormones, desire was always there; it was desire that led to all the touching and rubbing and endless naughtiness. But as we get older, desire is more a leap of faith—it's the touching that often comes first now, it's the actual physicality that generates the hormones and revs up desire into something frantically recognizable.

When I was pregnant I had lots of sexy dreams, but the reality of sex was harder to make happen. And yet I really wanted that closeness. Since I felt as if my body was off limits, I didn't mind putting all the focus on JB. Maybe I started off "faking" it, but I hesitate to use that word, because it was more like I was "open" to it. And the results were great. In that time, I discovered a new love for my man's little man.

Immodest sex maven I may be, but to be honest, I haven't historically been a huge fan of the penis. It's somewhat a visual thing, somewhat to do with cheap early encounters—but it's also just that "it" seemed so distant and bossy, especially with a million other things on my plate. "Blow job" too often implies just that—a job. "Giving head" does the same thing . . . giving giving giving. Where's the "get" here? Where's the "gimme"? But with my own gratification off the table, I was really able to fully be in the moment and explore his body without any preconceived notion of where it was supposed to go. Not to be all Mirabel Morgan about it, but there was something thrilling about focusing entirely on him that actually got me really hot. I started doing it for him, but it ended up being for me. And suddenly I saw his penis in an entirely new light . . . more like a kindly bald-headed hermit, coming out of his shell just for me, instead of some impersonal commando king. With a lot of mindfulness and a little imagination, I got my gimme, and was boldly taken where I really needed to go (out of my mind, out of my pregnant body and baby life) by a surprisingly sexy, empathetic commander, an ambassador to a vast universe that, in fact, looks quite a bit like that Captain Picard!

I'm More Game Than You Might Think (But I'm Not a Mind Reader)

There we were, naked in our neighbor's hot tub, and he's worried about someone seeing us. All I wanted was for him to attack me.

ALICIA, 25

Fellas, look. Just because we liked something you did one time ten years ago doesn't mean that's all she wrote. Similarly, if we nixed some new type of sex play, that doesn't mean it's off the table forever. (Unless we said, "hell no, that's off the table forever." Then, it probably is. . . .) People change, sex gets boring, body parts shift, emotional needs grow. We know that. If there's something you want to do, bring it up. Many times it might seem like we only like plain old boring get-it-on sex because, frankly, we're too tired to initiate something else. But that doesn't mean we're not open. If you bring something up, especially in a sweet and sexy way, you just might be surprised at how game we can be. Tell us what you like, what you need, what you want, what you've done in the past, what you wish you hadn't done, and what you're hoping to do to us. And sometimes just take a chance and attack us.

KAMA CHAMELEON: TIME FOR A CHANGE?

You don't have to whip out the *Kama Sutra* to realize that there are psychological dimensions to different positions. Depending on what you're looking for in any given sex session, it might be helpful to know that . . .

Around the world, the missionary position remains the most popular and most common, even though it's the one that's least likely to lead to female orgasm. Why does it remain so popular, and is often cited as a favorite amongst women? Maybe it's all that eye contact and sense of connectedness that comes with it.

Woman on top is the most consistently orgasmic for women, because it allows the women to achieve a high degree of clitoral friction and in a manner/pace that works for them. Studies have shown that women tend to fantasize more during sex than men (which makes sense as fantasy is a close cousin to dreaming and helps you to take a break from reality, let your brain deactivate, and let yourself go), while men tend to want to be visually stimulated during sex. Woman on top is certainly the position to provide that kind of feast for the eyes.

Doggie style: Sometimes it's just time to fuck, forget intimacy, forget love-making. This is all about hot, sweaty raw, animalistic fucking.

Side by side: Brings us back to the days of heavy petting: caressing, doting, kissing. Also easy for those of us who are getting soft in the middle and just want to be comfy, cozy, and all Sting-like and go all night. Side by side, we can focus on shallow thrusts, tune into each other's arousal arcs.

NOW YOU TRY IT
While "usual" is good and fine and fun, the next time you make love push yourself to try something new. Sometimes just a little change can make a big difference.

NAUGHTINESS: WHAT DADS WANT MOMS TO KNOW
I'm Bored (Un)Stiff

Sex just got so boring after having our baby. There was no spontaneity to it.

BEN, 33

Part of the problem for many couples in long-term relationships is that when it comes to sex, not unlike other aspects of our relationship, we become trapped in the same old routine sex scripts that map our behavior from foreplay to goodnight kiss. For most couples, sex becomes a rote, serial process. First comes kissing and hugging. This in turn leads to genital stimulation. That leads to intercourse and orgasm (nearly always his, hopefully hers). Same ol' thing, same ol' way. It's comfort-food sex; nice, cozy, goes down easy, and leaves us feeling full in the short-term. But we're not exactly bursting with anticipation for dessert, and before we know it we're feeling hunger pangs again. Maybe it's time to surprise us with something new, some spice. We're not talking "blowing things up" spice—there's real value in a foundation of familiarity. But give us a dash of something now and then to add a little heat.

When Did You Get So Lights Off in the Bedroom?

There's nothing more rewarding for a man than feeling *wanted* by a woman. Genuinely wanted. Having someone horny to pieces over you and able to show you.

SAM, 38

Truth is some of us are lights-on, others of us are lights-off, and here we are fighting over the dimmer switch. And we don't just mean that literally. Maybe we're sexually mismatched. When it comes to sexual compatibility, there are often two types: thrill seekers and comfort creatures. Thrill seekers crave a high degree of novelty and get bored very quickly, while comfort creatures believe that less is more. Part of the problem is that in the early stage of a relationship, the infatuation of falling in love provides a level of excitement that often masks real differences in our sexual types.

According to *Psychology Today*, one factor that may prove unifying or divisive to a couple is the degree to which their nervous systems are naturally inclined to pursue novel and stimulating experiences. Says Marvin Zuckerman, a psychologist at the University of Delaware: "A person's inherent need for sensation is not necessarily obvious in the early stages of a relationship, when love itself is a novelty and carries its own thrills—it's when the sex becomes routine that problems occur." While we may be sexually mismatched, or maybe there really are some fundamental differences in what we think of as good sex, we don't have to swing all the way to one side or the other. We can meet in the middle in a nice dimly lit room and both like it . . . but we won't ever know if we don't start talking about it.

In my work as a writer and sex therapist, I've talked to thousands of people about their sex lives. One thing I'm convinced of is that for most people the best sex they ever had is the best sex they "never" had: turn-ons, fantasies, hidden desires, stuff they're thinking about, but afraid to share for fear of being judged or thought weird by their partners, or even themselves. (Studies have shown that nearly one in two people feel guilty about their sexual fantasies, as they usually tap social and cultural taboos.) If we start sharing, maybe we'll find we're not as mismatched as we think we are, or that a little goes a long way. So let's start turning the "best sex never" into the "best sex ever." That starts with shedding some inhibitions and metaphorically turning up the lights—even just a little.

Case-study: Jake (35) was always hounding his wife, Chloe (31), to have a threesome, and then started in on wanting to swing with another couple. She thought he was a freak and was completely turned off by the idea. Especially now that she was a mom, she found herself increasingly angry at her husband's immature, "lewd" desires, and really thought it would break the marriage. Chloe didn't even want to indulge Jake in talk about his fantasies. But in my office I asked him to describe what turned him on and he spoke in very loving erotic language about how attracted he was to his wife, and how he wanted to watch her pleasured by another person, even if that other person was a man. Chloe had never thought that Jake was thinking of her satisfaction and pleasure, and it reassured her and turned her on to hear Jake talk like this. Two weeks later, they came back, happy and holding hands and seemed like newlyweds. They hadn't stopped talking about Jake's fantasy and it had led to some really hot sex. Chloe still wasn't interested in a threesome or swinging, but she was comfortable being more vocal about it, even talking about which friends she found hot or not. So it turned out that they weren't so sexually mismatched, and that fantasy didn't have to be turned into action. Moral of the story: When diving into the waters of fantasy, sometimes all you need to do is a dip a toe into the shallow end of the pool.

Have Love Map, Will Travel

Our love maps are our own unique sexual fingerprints. In other words, these "maps" represent the blueprint of our erotic desires, shaped by previous positive and negative sexual experiences and explaining everything from why we gravitate to a particular physical type to what feeds our private fantasies and actual practices. So where can these maps take you? Really, anywhere that tickles your fancy—and your fantasies.

As Kaye Wellings, a respected British sociobiologist and author, explains in her book *First Love, First Sex*, "Fantasies perform a valuable function. Most of us, most of the time, behave conservatively, sexually and otherwise. Our erotic experiences represent only the tip of the iceberg in terms of possibilities. Many possibilities only see the light of day through fantasies or dreams, seldom as reality." If you're the type of woman who feels lot of stress, whether about kids, the state of the house, or simply your inner mental chatter, then a little fantasy may be the key to deactivating those stress and anxiety centers. Is it in your love map? Try indulging a fantasy privately to get yourself in the mood or share a fantasy with your partner. Open the fantasy floodgates and watch your love maps carry you away.

Be Gentle with Me

Most of us guys grow up sexually on a steady diet of sexual misconceptions based on porn, pop culture, sound bites, and oh, yes, women who fake it. So it's no surprise that many of us can't tell good sex from bad and end up knowing more about what's under the hood of a car than a woman's clitoris. Too often we're expected to be sex gods in bed, but we don't even know what to do with that power! Beyond that, don't assume that just because we're quick on the draw or slow going that it's because we think it's what you want. Sometimes it just happens. Give us a pointer or two, but be gentle —while we crave feedback and guidance, criticism, expressed harshly, is the sexual kiss of death. As Kim Cattrall wrote of her own sex life in her book, *Satisfaction*, "premature ejaculators were the bane of my existence." Speaking as a guy, it's no fun to be the bane of anyone's existence, but a lot of women assume that if a guy is, er, trigger-happy, that he's sexually lazy or inconsiderate, when in fact he's suffering from a common sexual disorder that's extremely difficult to overcome.

Or Dominate Me

This is not an easy one for a guy (especially a father) to admit, since the journey to, and through, manhood is very much the journey of learning to stay in control. As R. Louis Schultz, M.D., wrote in his book, *Out in the Open: The Complete Male Pelvis*, "To live in society, we all require a degree of control. Too much control, however, and we can become automatons. Control is always being right. Control is not letting your feelings influence your life. Control is not letting the joy of life be a goal. Control is not expressing your feelings. Control is being neutral or neuter. Control is not being sensual. Control is lessening the enjoyment of sex. Control is not being aware or responsive to the feelings of others, since you are not aware of your own feelings. Control is always being on an even emotional plane." What's fascinating about this quote is not only was Dr. Schultz talking about the journey through manhood in general, but specifically how this sense of needing to be in control physically manifests in the male body, specifically the pelvic area. No surprise this area figures heavily in sexual desires and fantasies and is ultimately a region that signals a sense of letting go and surrender. From a fear of having his testicles roughhoused to sensitivity around the perineum (the area between testicles and anus that is rife with nerve endings and shields the male G-spot) to a "nobody touches me down there" attitude about his butt and anus, the male experience of sex is one that's controlled. So dominate us and help us give up some of the control and pressure to be in control that seems to go hand in hand with being a guy and a dad.

You Do Me, I'll Do You

For guys, there's often so much performance anxiety, or we worry about holding back and not letting go to passion during sex, it's a joy to sometimes be on the receiving end. Sometimes we just want to lie there and to be able to focus on those feelings and sensations, to indulge and be indulged. And as parents, there's often so little time or energy for sex that when we finally do get around to doing it, we're totally focused on mutual satisfaction. So give us that massage with a happy ending, and next time it will be your turn to receive. And maybe if we simplify our sex and take turns in the role of giver and receiver we can actually learn something new about each other. Also, make sure you're bringing your mindfulness skills to bed, ladies . . . literally. Focusing on your breath and paying attention to physical sensations can add depth and intensity to sex and sex play. Create the mood by getting in spoon position naked, lying down, with one of you holding the other from behind. Be still and synchronize your breathing. See what happens. It's not a huge move, but it can help you deactivate your mind, and activate your activity.

SEX RX FOR THE GUYS: LET'S TALK ABOUT SEX, BABY

It can be hard for us guys to open up about what we need and want. Here are some tips for getting the party started:

Do: just do it; talk about what you want—no one has ever actually died of embarrassment.

Do: say what you really want and need, the more specific the better; now is not the time to be coy.

Don't: talk about it when you're in the middle of a fight *or when you just didn't have sex.*

Do: think outside the box about sex; oral and manual sex count too.

Don't: label or generalize. ("You're a sex fiend." "You never want sex.")

Don't: think you can fix everything in one 45-minute discussion.

Do: let the other person know you love them.

SEX RX FOR THE LADIES: TREASURE MAP = PLEASURE MAP

One of the best ways to understand what makes us tick sexually, or to tap into our love maps, is to reflect on erotically memorable experiences and our early fantasies, especially those that have survived in some measure over time and form

a core sense of erotic identity. Think about your most erotically memorable experience (or experiences) and make a list
of them. Remember, we're talking about erotically memorable, not necessarily sexually memorable. Maybe the experience didn't actually involve sex, or orgasm, or only involved
sexual interaction up to a point. Maybe a strong flirtation
was your most erotically memorable experience, or an intense sense of sexual anticipation. Maybe it was a smoldering
passion that was highly charged but sexually unrequited.
You probably have more sexual thoughts than you give yourself credit for. For example, thirty-three-year-old Janet considered herself a person who never thought about sex. She
was too busy being the mother of two. And yet, when she
made her list during the day she was surprised to find that
she thought about sex way more than she had previously realized. The thought didn't necessarily make her want to have
sex, but it gave her a sense of erotic stirring. This is what
we're going for! Instead of blocking these instances out
(which as busy parents is probably your MO), start thinking
about them. Let your mind wander. If you feel you haven't
had an erotically memorable experience, focus on a time
when you felt an almost overwhelming pull of attraction
and/or desire, something that seemed to come up in your
fantasies time and again. Or maybe it was a scene in a movie
or a passage in a book that left an indelible stamp on your
sexual psyche.

After making your list, spend another day paying extra

attention to the things that turned you on. What triggered them? Are there certain sounds or smells that turn you off or on? Are you a visual person, or do you respond more to sound or scent? You might be surprised to find you're more sexual than you think.

The Naughty Mommy's Naughty Moment: Heidi

There's one sexual experience in my love map that I still look back on, and it involved no actual sex. It was before I met JB; I had just moved to San Francisco, and I was young and lonely in the big city. One day I was riding a crowded city bus; it was summer and it was hot. I remember trying to get my balance, with nothing to hold onto, when the bus lurched forward and threw me into the guy in front of me. Though we were surrounded by people, suddenly it was like we were the only two people in the world. I could feel every inch where our bodies touched; I could smell his heat, hear his breathing and feel the tension in his body as it spoke to mine. When the bus pulled away and we all lurched back, I didn't move, and neither did he. We stayed there, pressed up against each other as intimate strangers, thrilled, excited, and wet with way more than just sweat. Even now, I get hot when I think of that experience. When JB and I have been fighting about not having sex, or I find myself feeling like a big loser because I'd rather watch Biggest Loser than fool around, I think of that day on the bus and remember that I really am a sexual person. Just a really tired one.

SEX RX TO DO TOGETHER:
LET'S TRAVEL THE FOUR POLES OF FANTASY

A big part of exploring our love maps is to not be ashamed of what interests us. Sigmund Freud gave fantasy a bad name back in 1908 when he said, "A happy person never fantasizes, only a dissatisfied one." Granted, this is also the guy who said clitoral orgasms were immature, and fortunately, we've had a century of research (and impassioned women) to prove Freud wrong. The truth is, a healthy fantasy life is one key to a great sex life—and your partner might not always play the leading role. Fantasy isn't the sad daydreaming of the lonely, forlorn, or frustrated in love. Research shows that people with active fantasy lives are more sexually satisfied, more sexually responsive, and more adventurous about sex in general. Not bad.

Once we've got our love map we can travel the four poles: exhibitionism, voyeurism, domination, submission. Let's go where we haven't gone before. Nobody's saying we have to dive into the deep end, but let's at least dip our toes in together.

- *Exhibitionism:* Does the idea of being watched turn you on? Have you ever engaged in any acts of exhibitionism: from skinny-dipping, to having loud sex, to having sex outdoors, to making a sex tape? What would be an exhibitionistic fantasy that, while pushing your comfort zone, you might do under the right circumstances? What's your safe, sexy danger zone? Write down one exhibitionistic turn-on and one turnoff. Maybe getting it on in a changing room at a department store is your cup of tea, but making a sex tape isn't? Many couples have played in the sexual currents of fantasy without being sure how much deeper they are willing to go. Here's one way: Make a sex tape without actually turning on the camera—it turns out it's often just as much fun, and as much of a turn-on, to plan the script together.

- *Voyeurism:* Do you like to watch? If you looked outside your window and saw two people having sex in a window across the way, would you avert your eyes or reach for binoculars? Do you have a fantasy of watching your partner get it on with someone else while you watch? What are some of your voyeuristic fantasies? Are there any you'd like to explore? What's your safe, sexy danger zone?

- *Domination and submission:* From ropes and a smack on the butt to sex in positions that exploit the helplessness of your lover, where do your tastes lie? What's your safe, sexy danger zone? As an example, a woman may be turned on by the idea of tying up her husband and teasing and tantalizing him into submission with oral sex, but turned off by the idea of any sort of spanking or violence.

IN CONCLUSION

Maybe it's inevitable, maybe familiarity really does breed sexual boredom. It's so darn easy to take sex for granted, to fall into sexual mediocrity with your best friend, who also happens to be your one and only sexual partner. But maybe that boredom is really just a bump, a step, a ramp to take off from. Maybe this hurdle is enough of a push to send you flying on a new path of discovery, to chart a whole new out-of-this-world course on your shared love map. Maybe it can help you uncover what's always been there, buried under a boring gray suit of responsibility: uncharted territory where you really can have it all—naughtiness and nice kids, sensuality and security, friendship and fucking. It's a bird, it's a plane, it's . . . the supermom of sex lives, and there's no (good) reason it can't be yours.

S/M: SUCCESS IN THE SUBURBS
• • • **Jane Black** • • •

My second-grade daughter is rummaging around in my bathroom drawer (as second-grade daughters sometimes do) and she makes a rather unfortunate discovery. She wanders out of the bathroom holding a small butt plug, and asks, "What's this, Mommy?"

Yikes. Guess we forgot to put it back in the toy box last night. "Well, sweetie, it's, umm, well, it's . . . it's a pacifier. For

---

the baby." Fortunately, I actually have a baby, so this explanation is not completely implausible. I continue folding clothes on the bed, surreptitiously looking at her to see if she's buying it. She is. This is good, because if she follows up by asking anything else (for example, "Wouldn't this thing choke the little guy?") I'll be hard pressed to keep on going.

"Can you put it back, please?" I ask her casually, and she obediently puts it in the drawer. I make a note to myself to put it back where it belongs later, when she's not around. Back in the toy box right next to the wrist and ankle cuffs, the dildos, the blindfolds, the collars, the harnesses, the nipple clamps, the rope, the whips, the hood, the corsets, and the ball gag.

In most ways, we're a traditional family: one mom, one dad, married to each other, raising their biological kids in a house in the suburbs. My husband and I both have master's degrees, though I quit my job a few years ago to be a stay-home mom. Like a million other dads, he schleps off to a white-collar job every weekday. I shuttle the kids around in our silver minivan, I make peanut butter sandwiches, I vacuum Cheerios off the floor, I play Candyland.

I play other games, too.

The first time my husband kissed me, he grabbed a fistful of my hair, pulled my head backward uncomfortably far, and held me there—suspended in time and confused, aroused, uneasy. He bent his head over mine and bit my lip, hard. I'd never been treated this way. Some little area of my brain that had been dormant suddenly came rocketing awake—and it turned out that this rocket was connected directly to my crotch.

We fucked at least once or twice a day every day for the next year. We spent over a thousand dollars on all manner of toys, latex, and leather. We played out progressively more S/M-oriented scenes, pushing our boundaries, exploring what worked and what didn't. We spanked, whipped, clamped, and tied. We fell in love and got married.

We both wanted a family, so we made some babies. Three of them. They're cute little things, our kids, and we love them utterly, but they create challenges for our sex life. There's the libido-killing sleep deprivation after each baby is born, of course. All parents have to deal with this. But even after the sleeplessness eases up, sex is still tricky for us, because S/M takes more time—and more privacy—than vanilla sex.

By necessity, vanilla quickies have become the staple of our sex life. Quickies are good. Quickies are fun. But they aren't enough. S/M brings a level of closeness between us that is in an entirely different category. It's how I tell him that I am still completely his, and how he tells me that he still completely wants me. Playing out an S/M scene colors our relationship for days—and sometimes weeks—afterward. The afterglow lasts much longer than it does with vanilla sex. We're more gentle with each other. We touch each other more. We laugh more. We're more patient with the kids.

Perhaps ironically, the more time I spend being a mother, the more I crave the release of an intense scene. I want to shrug off that part of me that's always on duty, watching over my children and protecting them, and put myself entirely in my lover's power. The fact is, being a mindless sex slave—relinquishing all volition, abandoning conscious thought for awhile—can be pretty therapeutic.

We still do S/M, but we've made some adjustments. Chains, for example, are too loud—these days, we limit ourselves to ropes. And I can't wear nipple clamps when I'm lactating. Some adjustments have to be more subtle. I am often unable to put myself into the mind-set that's needed to engage in some of the more intense activities. I can be submissive, but I can't sink completely down into that dark, mindless, helpless place when I know that I could be interrupted at any time by a big kid having a bad dream, by a little kid needing a cup of water, by a baby needing to be rocked back to sleep.

For the most part we just work around the challenges. Every now and again we get Grandma to stay with the kids overnight so that we can go to a hotel and have some real private time together. Like lots of other people, we're willing to pay for sex—it's just that in our case, the money goes to Marriott. We hand the minivan keys to the valet, we lug in our duffel bag of toys, and we hang up the Do Not Disturb sign. It doesn't always work out, but when it does, it lights our marriage on fire.

The emotional connection we establish through S/M is an essential component of our relationship. Only my husband can touch that part of me, only he knows it's even there. I'm wearing T-shirts with spit-up stains and I'm carting around a diaper bag and I'm a soccer mom in a minivan. But I'm also, every now and again, a slave. It's part of what makes our marriage work, and it's part of what makes our family work—though with any luck, the kids will never know it.

DIAGNOSE THIS!
THE NEWLYBED GAME

Couples, go on down . . . oops, we mean come on down! It's your turn to play the NewlyBED game. So you've started a new family—well, now it's time to get a new start . . . in bed (or the kitchen, or the car, or whatever kid-free space you can find). Don't be shy, and don't lie; now is the time for some serious sharing. Remember, the only thing you have to lose is your libidos. Consider this your foreplay homework. Give yourself five points each time players 1 and 2 match answers:

1a. The right number of times per week for player 1 to make love is:

Player 1 _____ Player 2 _____

1b. The right number of times per week for player 2 to make love is:

Player 2 _____ Player 1 _____

2a. I can tell when player 2 is really having fun in bed because:

2b. I can tell when player 1 is really having fun in bed because:

3a. The most exciting foreplay for player 1 is:

3b. The most exciting foreplay for player 2 is:

4a. Something player 2 would never do in bed is:

4b. Something player 1 would never do in bed is:

5a. Something new player 1 wants or would be willing to try is:

5b. Something new player 2 wants or would be willing to try is:

6a. Player 2's honest to goodness favorite sexual position is:

6b. Player 1's honest to goodness favorite sexual position is:

7a. The (most) sure bet time of the day (or night) to hit on player 1 is:

7b. The (most) sure bet time of the day (or night) to hit on player 2 is:

8a. The sexiest body part of player 2 (besides "sexy bits") is:

8b. The sexiest body part of player 1 (besides "sexy bits") is:

9a. The part of player 2's body that would like more attention from player 1 (anywhere goes):

9b. The part of player 1's body that would like more attention from player 2 (anywhere goes):

10a. The ideal way for player 1 to wrap up lovemaking is:

10b. The ideal way for player 2 to wrap up lovemaking is:

Score!

0–35: It's all fun and games . . . wait . . . where's the fun? Where's the games? And how can you know if you don't talk about it a little more often? There's so much to keep learning about each other. Sex is not a dirty word—it's a fun word and even more fun to do when you know how to better share it with your partner.

40–75: Well, we've got some nice parting gifts for you—but hopefully with a little more communication like this you can give your partner a few more gifts . . . in bed.

80–100: Winner! Congratulations! Communication abounds. Keep it up (and keep it UP)!

CHAPTER SEVEN

Slumping It: Torn by Porn, Flirty Friendships, Unfair Fighting, and Other Things Your Relationship Is Vulnerable to When You're Not Having Sex

LIGHTS, CAMERA . . . ACTION?

It's sleepover night! Which means Mom and Dad are alone together for twenty-four kid-free hours, in the comfort of their own home. Within minutes, however, they're each doing their own thing. Afraid of more fighting, they don't even bring up sex; it's now an off-limits topic. They skate through the niceties of the day, like roommates or once-close-but-not-anymore-friends, then head to their respective activities: Mom to the gym to work out (aka, bitch about her life and flirt with her pilates instructor), Dad to the office to work (aka, check out porn and chat with his online female "friends"). This dry spell has become a real slump—and it's only getting harder to get out.

IAN: *Okay, Heidi, pop quiz?*

HEIDI: *Let's do it!*

IAN: *Masturbating to porn—cheating or not?*

HEIDI: *Not, unless you're going to call my cheesy romance novels cheating too.*

IAN: *A flirty friendship that your spouse doesn't know about? Cheating or not?*

HEIDI: *Danger! Danger! Not cheating, but a slippery slope for sure.*

IAN: *Going to a strip club? Cheating or not?*

HEIDI: *Rrrr. I don't like it. I guess it's not cheating, but cheap thrills at a high cost. I'd rather JB wanted to watch me strip.*

IAN: *Massage with happy ending? Cheating or not?*

HEIDI: *Cheaty. Anything with touch + fluids = totally not cool. Do those even really exist? I just want the massage . . .*

IAN: *Thinking about another person during sex? Cheating or not?*

HEIDI: *Does that new James Bond guy count? Definitely not cheating, or I'm like totally busted.*

IAN: *Getting drunk and kissing someone other than your spouse under the mistletoe?*

HEIDI: *On the lips? No spouse in sight? WAAAY out of bounds. Calling her the next day? Cheating.*

IAN: *Well, you're a hell of a lot looser than Lisa on this stuff. I'd be kicked to the stoop on the strip club, and served with divorce papers on the massage with happy ending.*

HEIDI: *I think it comes down to trust. We all draw lines at different places, but the common denominator is trust. Instead of sneaking out and going, I'd rather JB came to me and said, "Man, I just really* *want to go to a strip club," and talked to me about why: what he gets from it, what he's not getting from our sex life, and so on. For that matter, I wouldn't be stoked AT ALL about it (Hear me, JB ? UN-STOKED), but if he really really really wanted to see what a massage with a happy ending was like, I wouldn't automatically shut him down . . . as long as he talked to me about it, included me in it, opened up to me about his wants. For me, the trust we build and share is more important than the details of what we do. It's that same sense of trust that is essential for a happy sex life. We're not going to try new things, or push our collective sexual limits if there is not a serious trust base there. With nothing to hide, there's really nothing to hide . . . meaning we open to each other fully and explicitly in a way we can't do with just anyone else.*

> **Sooner or later things come to a head. They rebel and find sex elsewhere: online, or in flings, tricks, or affairs. Or they leave, even if that means waiting till the kids grow up. Or they stay, but grow so bitter and resentful that you'd wish they'd leave.**
>
> **ESTHER PEREL, *MATING IN CAPTIVITY***

> **My bitterness with my husband grew—soon there just wasn't anything left in the sex department for him.**
>
> **TIANA, 43**

So far we've talked about some hard stuff, some funny stuff, and some basic know-how. But here's the real tough stuff. This chapter is for those for whom "Let's get it on" have become real fighting words. It's for those of us who are dangerously turned off by our partners and tuning in to other things or other people. It's for those who have a late-night user ID like "sexy-dad1" or "hungrymama." It's for those of us who stonewall the other, who shut out any communication on the topic and hope things will just get better on their own. Or who resign ourselves to a sexless marriage. It's for those of us who find ourselves in a no fun cycle of withdrawing and withholding, or who are bitter and resentful. Or those who may have even given up altogether, saying with a sigh, "Oh well, I never liked sex much anyway," or "Maybe it's okay if we're just roommates. . . ." *But it's not okay.* Like we said in the introduction, sex does matter. It fuels us, even when we forget how much. It keeps us going when things get rough, it gives us a spark to keep things fired up in lives that otherwise can get quite chilly.

> He's so frustrated with me that I never initiate it or try to do fun, alternative things, and I'm not passionate. He takes it very personally and keeps saying, "Why don't we just be friends and raise two kids together? That's how we are now."
>
> REBECCA, 27

> Our friends fight behind closed doors and say, "We should be more like the _____s!!!" not realizing that while we have a very "functional" marriage, we're emotionally disconnected.
>
> PHILLIP, 42

SLUMPING: WHAT MOMS WANT DADS TO KNOW
We Do Think About Sex—Just Not with You

I got together with my husband as a hot 25-year-old and suddenly I'm a stay-at-home mom checking out the dads at the park.

LISA, 27

We know sometimes it seems as if we don't care about sex at all. But it's more that we don't care about sex with you. As harsh as that sounds, it's hard to like sex with you when we don't like you. It's not that we dislike you, it's that we don't like you with a capital *L*. Too much fighting and sexual stalemating leaves us feeling . . . stale. Some of us have gotten to the point where it feels like you're just not adding anything to the equation here. We need some attention—some real attention, because if we don't get it from you we'll start thinking about getting it from the UPS guy we see every day. Again, we get locked into these old roles and stop seeing each other as lovers, as complex human beings far beyond just Mom and Dad. But look hard, "Dad." It's not easy to see sometimes, but there's a woman under here, the same one you fell in love with once. You just have to dig a little to find her.

Cheating Is Cheating—That Goes for Emotional Stuff, Too

It's all sneaky and creepy and the emotional cheating is as bad as the physical. It's awful to think of you getting together with someone else, but it's almost just as awful to imagine you sharing what you're really thinking with someone else. You might think flirting is harmless, but if you take it too far, even if nothing physical happens, it feels cheaty to us. We're hungry for you. Maybe not sexually all the time, but emotionally. Other women might seem like they have none of the same problems, that they're interested in you in a new and exciting way, but really, this is where the action really is. Let's get through this and start seeing each other in that light again.

We had an "incident" once when JB was out of town and he went to a strip club with some male coworkers. Even though he and I have gone to strip clubs together before, I really felt betrayed. It wasn't the money, which was obscene in itself, but the fact that he hid it from me. (Like I wouldn't notice? How much can dinner with the guys really cost?) I felt it was way off limits, even though if I were there it would have been different. The fact of the matter is, he had a sexual experience with other women, without me, and kept it from me—and it stung.

This affair/flirty-relationship/playing-with-fire thing swings both ways, of course. There was a time when I was taking flirty friendships too far. And yes, my daughter's swim instructor may have been super cute—but in truth he wasn't what I wanted at all. What I wanted was an escape from my boring life and petty arguments, and my tame role as "Mom." When I think about it now, I can see what I really wanted was an affair with my husband—but my pre-baby, pre-marriage, pre-boring-fight-over-everything-lately husband. I just wanted to stop experiencing everything as a "duty" and start living a passionate life again with the man I really love. In retrospect, the swim instructor's really got nothin' on my husband. He was just there while I happened to be going through my own questions. But isn't there always someone there, always something to use as an excuse if you're really looking for one?

My wife says having a flirty friendship is cheating. I don't get it: It's not like I'm having sex. Cheating involves sex with someone else, no two ways about it.

TERRANCE, 33

Fighting All the Time Sucks

C'mon, we want to make love, not WAAH! And despite what it looks like most evenings around 6 p.m., I'm actually a lover, not a fighter! For a wedding gift our dear old roommate gave JB and me a framed Bruce Lee movie poster that says across the top, in big letters: "Best Fight Scene." We had many fights in front of him, and he admired the way we went at it—the way we never made him feel so uncomfortable that he had to leave. Or maybe because we lived with other people we learned how to fight in a better way—we retained a level of civility we might not have if we were alone and didn't know someone was watching. I think we should always fight like that—as if someone is watching. It keeps things from exploding. That's useful now, too, because our little ones are watching. Sure, we don't want them to think that everything's easy all the time because that's unrealistic. But we also want them to learn how to argue in a fair way that shows we still love each other.

I Love You and I Want to Work Things Out

We said "I do" to each other once before, and we're saying it now. We DO want to make things better. We DO love you. We DO think we can work this out. Let's stop trying to figure out who's to blame, where the "real problem" lies. Let's let go of anger and reach out to each other with compassion instead. Help us break out of it—take a chance, a leap of faith, and do something totally out of character. Reach out, share, pull us to you instead of walking away. And we'll do the same.

SLUMPING: WHAT DADS WANT MOMS TO KNOW

I'm (Not Really) Tuned Out and Turned Off

Here's the truth: Sometimes we're lying when we say we're just not feeling sexual. We say we're stressed out, tired, there's nothing wrong, we're just not feeling up to it. We say it's us, not you, but really . . . it is you. It's not that we're not feeling desire, we're just not feeling it for you. If your guy says he's just not feeling sexual, it's a call to action, not a reason to go on accepting this state of diminished expectations. Sure it's sometimes easier to think there's nothing wrong and leave it at that, but how many times have you said nothing's wrong and really meant the exact opposite? The same is true of guys, even more so, when you think about how hard it is for us to talk about sex and relationships. Just like faking it, we don't want to deal or let on or hurt your feelings. So when we say we're just not feeling sexual, don't take that as a conversation stopper, use it as a conversation starter—to start to figure out what's really going on.

> **My husband of ten plus years (and father of four) isn't remotely interested in sex anymore. Sometimes we've gone months without. He doesn't even want to discuss it with me, so I just let it go.**
>
> CELISE, 37

Come on, It's Just a Little Porn . . .

For the most part, masturbation is a normal, healthy part of sexuality. And even more a part of it when we're not getting any elsewhere. And porn is a little bit like gun control—we should mainly be concerned with the state of mind of the people pulling the trigger. If we're feeling tuned out and turned off, porn becomes a way of escaping from the relationship rather than just a harmless way to blow off some sexual steam. What did we say earlier about guys always thinking about sex, and those thoughts triggering little jolts of desire that we're compelled to gratify? Guys tend to rely a lot on external triggers like porn to get the blood flowing, whereas it seems women often resort to internal triggers. And with the ready availability of porn online, it's easy for a guy to start going down a slippery slope to the point where porn has replaced his erotic imagination. When porn wasn't so readily available, we were forced to search our own history of erotically memorable experiences and flip through that collection of fantasies we'd accumulated. In short, to get in touch with our love maps. With the easy access of the Internet, though, some of us have developed a dependence on the stuff. While porn addiction is the subject of clinical debate, more and more professionals are agreeing that it's a real problem. In the brain's search for quick gratification you can become just as habituated to it as a drug, and it's easier to start feeling as if you need more and more of it. It starts to become a self-perpetuating, somewhat mind-numbing, and soul-deadening experience.

If you think your guy is in need in of a break from porn, don't be confrontational. Instead, approach the situation constructively. It's too easy to let yourself get hijacked by anxiety, fear, panic, and uncertainty: "What does this mean to our relationship?" "Is this what he's really into?" "How can I compete?" or "How long has this been going on?" Think about everything we've discussed and realize that in this case as well, you need to talk about things constructively. Talk to him about his sexual desires in a way that's positive and sexy. Engage his erotic imaginations and expand both your love maps from the inside out. A porn problem doesn't have to be the end of the road; it can be the start of an erotic transformation in your relationship.

I once counseled a guy who felt that his wife was inhibited in bed and had discovered a world of fantasy and kink in an online chat room, where he had started an intoxicating dialogue with a woman called NastyGirl69. He hadn't met her in person, but these conversations illuminated how much was lacking in his marriage. His wife was a great friend and a great mother, but she just didn't understand his essence the way NG69 did. He decided he was going to talk to her, and next week he came in all torn up. He had started to tell his wife, and she angrily retorted that she knew all about NastyGirl69—she knew all about her, because she was her—she'd been snooping on his online patterns for a while, and while he was off in the den supposedly working, she was surreptitiously logging online as well and having the kind of conversation that he considered inappropriate to the wife and mother of his children.

It was their own modern version of the "Piña Colada" song, but without the hummable chorus and happy ending. He was furious with his wife: She'd been snooping on him, she'd humiliated him, even though he'd been sneaking around too. They ended up coming in together and working through the anger. She admitted that at first she'd simply been snooping and logged on to see what he was into. She was shocked, and felt like he'd been cheating on her, but a couple of her friends told her to get over it. The next time she went online she actually found herself enjoying the conversation with her husband and realized that what she really wanted was to be recognized for the nasty girl that resided within her.

I wish he would have an affair—at least he'd stop bothering me for sex.

DORA, 39

Go Ahead, Snoop on Me!

Honestly, we shouldn't have anything to hide in the first place. This isn't a blank check to start snooping on your partner and reading emails and Internet visits. However, if your partner is saying everything is fine, but your Spidey Sense is tingling, you owe it to yourself to figure it out. If you do snoop and you don't discover anything, that's a reason to start looking into the other parts of the relationship that aren't working. A lot of people who do snoop end up finding something that makes them feel uncomfortable, but that might just be something worth talking about.

I was once interviewed on CNN and said it was okay to snoop, so Lisa went and snooped through my emails and found some stuff that she didn't like. Personally, I didn't think it was emotional infidelity or even a flirtation, but she was upset about a relationship with a colleague, and that allowed us to talk. I didn't like the idea that she'd been snooping, but the truth is that Lisa was also pregnant with our second son at the time, and rather than being connected we were pretty disconnected. So having a sparkly, energetic friendship with a colleague of the opposite sex was the straw that broke the camel's back—fortunately, not her water. For me it was just an intellectually engaging friendship, but Lisa felt the woman was strongly attracted to me and interested in more than being just friends.

You have to remember that there are two people involved. Being able to see your partner's point of view and validate his or her emotions without jumping to the conclusion that your partner is jealous, is important. And as I'm sure Heidi and Lisa would say to me, "'Sparkly' friendship? Ian! That's called flirting, silly."

It's true, some of us men never get it when a woman is hot for us. But here's something we can and should see coming: If a guy has a female friend who is always asking, "Oh, what's the matter?" and he's confiding to her about this fight or that problem with his wife, that's a sign. Because when you talk to friends of the opposite sex about your relationship problems, there's a problem developing in your relationship!

I Admit It—Sometimes It's Easier to Be at Work Than Here with You

At the office things make sense. People don't fight with me, they don't have crazy hormones. And I'm good at what I do there. Here . . . too often I feel like I can't do anything right. Many of us guys are more sensitive than we look or act. All this tension, this fighting about sex, this endless talking about "our relationship" wears us out and brings us down—physically and emotionally. It makes us a little limp. Sometimes it's just easier to hide out at the office than deal with real life. And yet we want you. We don't want to wait until the kids are grown to get your affection back. We want it—we need it—now more than ever.

I'm Not So Bad After All;
Other Women Still Smile at Me
(Especially When I'm Out with the Baby)

Every time I read or hear about deadbeat dads, I find myself thinking, hey I'm not so bad, I'm still here. That's better than my dad ever did. I mean, I could be that guy with the hot young girlfriend.

RAY, 45

There's nothing wrong with a little bit of flirting; not only is it human, it adds to the richness of life and can contribute to the richness of our relationship. In the best of circumstances, we flirt a little bit, we make eye contact, we chat somebody up a bit and it gives our self-esteem a little boost and adds to our lust for life, and frankly lust for you. But when the sexual connection with our partner is closed off and shut down, we become vulnerable to infidelity and start to seek out these little flirty jolts of connection with greater intensity. We start to think we're not so bad after all, and many men start to build the internal logic for taking things further. Like lawyers we start to build our case and rationalize to defend our behaviors. Ultimately, this is a cop out. It's too easy to seek outside our relationship rather than search within it. Sure, you're not so bad after all, but before you start justifying a cycle of steadily increasing bad behavior and pinning the blame on your wife and kids, consider that you might be one step away from actually becoming that bad—and take responsibility for your own actions.

I Love You and I Want to Work Things Out

It's not easy for guys to always say it, but here it is: We love you and care about you and want sex to be a part of our lives. Or we wouldn't be reading this book, right? Sometimes we get so caught up in the battles, in the bad stuff, in the hard stuff we forget to let you know this basic point. So here it is again: We love you. We want things to be better. Here we are. Let's talk (not bitch, not blame, not nag). Just talk.

SEX RX FOR THE LADIES: MAKE A LIST, CHECK IT TWICE

As baby brouhahas and other wily woes hit your relationship, it's all too easy to see (and blame) your partner's flaws. Here's an easy exercise to help you start seeing your guy in a more loverly light, to remember why you love him and to check in with yourself about what you're choosing to focus on. The first step is to list as many things as you can remember about your partner that turned you on when you first met. Some of them may no longer be applicable—no matter, write it all down and we'll worry about that later.

For instance, here's Heidi's list about JB:

1. mellow, grounded
2. musical, creative
3. super smart, great debater, passionate about fairness, justice, etc.
4. hot—of course! olive skin, sexy bones
5. made me laugh
6. wounded
7. didn't sweat small stuff
8. responsible
9. totally devoted to me, believed in me completely
10. single-focused

Now, make a list of new positives you've discovered as well. For instance, Heidi's might be:

1. amazing, engaged dad
2. loves my family/my family loves him
3. supports us financially so I can stay home with kids
4. is so totally cool about me writing shamelessly about our sex life!

Of course, over the years you may have noticed some negative attributes as well. Find and add these to your list, as Heidi has below:

1. argues easily and loudly (feels like bullying)
2. incapable of multitasking
3. doesn't see dirt or bills
4. never lets me off the hook about things
5. moody/asshole sometimes
6. tired a lot, doesn't try to inspire me

Now it's time to look over your lists. Think about which positive statements are still true. Looking at your own list of positive and negative attributes, think about how the negatives have gotten in the way of experiencing the positives.

As I looked over my list, what was really interesting to me was how most of the positive statements I wrote about JB were still true. The problem is, while they were charming when we were younger, they kind of conspire to be a pain in my ass now; really, most of the negatives I listed are connected to the positives. For instance, I liked JB being single-focused, as long as he was focusing on me. I don't like when it means he can't see the chores that need to be done because he's focusing on the kids (or a football game). Similarly, I used to love his passion for arguing—but I sure don't when he's arguing with me.

Doing this exercise has helped me think about things in two ways. First and foremost, I just felt a surge of love for him while going over the "early positives." He really is a remarkable person, even if he is a moody butt sometimes! Second, it was great to think of the attributes I generally put in "bad" or "good" categories just in the "JB" category. When we got married we promised to love each other "with all that we have and all that we are." This is who he is. I can't just take the good side of what's there—it's a package deal. I can't get all sappy and sloppy with the "wounded" little boy I fell in love with but miss the real-life wounded grown man who actually has some issues too. I can't appreciate his faith in me, but whine when he doesn't let me off easy. That doesn't mean I can't expect certain things from him, or try to help him grow and heal some of those things. But it does mean reminding myself that I married a real human, as he did, and to remember that the good and the bad go hand in hand. I'm not always perfect either (I know, I know, it's hard to believe . . .) and I want him to give my "quirks" (annoying behavior) the benefit of the doubt too.

Sometimes, by simply shifting the way we look at our partner's attributes we can change the way we respond to them. By seeing the whole picture and focusing on the positives, we can become more tolerant and gentle with each other when we need it the most.

SEX RX FOR THE GUYS: ARE YOU GETTING TOO GRAPHIC WITH YOUR GRAPHICS?

Figure out if you have a porn problem, and give yourself a chance to detox:

- Do you always masturbate with porn? Have you become reliant on external visual stimulation as opposed to your own imagination or memories?

- After you masturbate to porn, do you find yourself recharged and relieved or bummed out and lonely?
- Do you use porn because you're sexually frustrated in your relationship?
- Are you relying on porn more and more frequently?
- Is your use of porn tapping you out erotically, leaving little to nothing for your partner?
- Are you spending too much money on porn sites?
- Is your use of porn getting in the way of work or other day-to-day responsibilities?
- Do you think about pornographic images/scenes when you're actually having sex?
- Do you feel a pressure to perform like a porn star?
- Do you judge your partner's sexual performance based on images from porn?
- Do you use porn to escape from issues in the way that one might abuse drugs or alcohol?
- Is your use of porn an entirely solo activity, or do you share it with your partner?
- Are you hiding your use of porn from your partner?

If you answered yes to most of these questions, you might be a developing a porn problem. Give yourself a porn break: Spend a full thirty days off porn, and let yourself detoxify. It might be hard at first, and you may want to be particularly vigilant when it comes to time alone at the computer. But you'll also be amazed at how quickly you can start to redirect your erotic resources into your relationship.

SEX RX TO DO TOGETHER: FIGHT CLUB

More and more research indicates that it's not what we argue about that matters as much as *how* we argue—our approach to confrontation can exact as big a toll on our health as other factors such as diet and exercise. Arguing naturally triggers the brain's "fight or flight" response system. Many men respond by fighting, and it's been shown that this confrontational approach raises one's heart rate, increases blood pressure, and plays a big role in cardiac disease. But interestingly, the opposite reaction, flight, can be just as harmful, if not worse, to women. It leads to self-silencing: a bottling up of emotions that causes anxiety, depression, and a cascade of unhealthy behaviors. Not surprisingly, sex is one main reason people argue, often above money, housework, and other common sources of conflict. Partners tend to keep bottled up about sex because they're afraid of eliciting an angry reaction. You can be lying in bed next to someone and feel a million miles apart.

Even when you're fighting against each other, when you're a couple, there's an us-against-the-world mentality that you need to maintain. Your partner is the person who shares your bed, and you have to defend that bond from outside forces. Knowing that no matter what, your partner is the one person who believes in you and will always be there for you can make all of the difference in the world when you

argue. Here are some tips for fighting that can help you remember that.

- **Hate (and other strong words) is a four-letter word.**
  Using the word *hate* or other strong, judgmental words
  is bad because it doesn't help convey understanding.
  Never say "I hate your friends" or "I hate your parents." You should be honest, but you need to be cool
  about it. Instead you can say things like "I'm uncomfortable about this" or "I know you love your parents,
  but sometimes they . . ." and then name something
  specific.
- **Be positive and constructive.** Here's a tip when you
  want to be honest and constructive. Start with "instead." Such as, "Instead of your mother coming over
  here, why don't you have a mom's night out?"
- **Provide tangible examples.** It can be hard in the heat of
  the moment, but this is important. It keeps things real
  and gives us something to work on.
- **Use I statements.** Start with "I feel" instead of "You
  make me . . ."
- **Fight fair.** This means don't attack or hit below the belt.
  You know what we mean.

Therapist John Gottman has spent a lifetime working
with married couples, researching what makes some marriages succeed and others fail. Gottman concluded, "It's the

balance between positive and negative emotional interactions in a marriage that determines its well-being—whether the good moments of mutual pleasure, passion, humor, support, kindness, and generosity outweigh the bad moments of complaining, criticism, anger, disgust, contempt, defensiveness, and coldness." Those couples that succeed in their marriages enjoy an overriding proportion of positive over negative sentiment. But, how do you ensure that? "All couples, happy and unhappy, have conflict, but the ratio of positive to negative interactions during arguments is a critical factor," and Gottman proposed that this ratio should, ideally, be 5 to 1. While it's impossible to go through life tallying positive versus negative interactions, it is possible to determine intuitively whether your relationship is generally in the positive, or tending more toward the negative. And then you can change it.

IN CONCLUSION

It doesn't take much for small sex problems to become big sex problems over time. But this is where it stops. This is where you gamble everything on love, and you put all your chips in for real. This is where your start talking, you open up, you turn off the fake and easy turn-ons the world has to offer, and opt to take on the big, hard life issues instead. This is where you grow, this is where you learn, you push through. It's where you give up looking for mythical pots of gold and relationship four-leaf clovers and instead do the real work you need to make your own luck and sexy scores. That's where you find the charm in long-term relationships, that's the sweet spot, the end of the rainbow, the good stuff that keeps it all so "magically delicious."

A Beautiful Compromise

LIGHTS, CAMERA . . . ACTION?

Picture this: A couple in their fifties are taking a road trip to visit their oldest kid at college. As they drive their sporty and practical new Euro-van, they laugh at the bumper sticker their kids gave them that says, "If this van is rockin' don't come a knockin". They chat, they share, they argue (nicely) over talk radio, and then change the channel only to find "their song" playing. As they sing along, they pass a rest stop sign and sneak naughty looks at each other. Dad signals safely and off they go, parking like the old days. In a corner of the rest stop, they close the shades and undress giggling nervously. They take time to appreciate each other's bodies, which have changed so much. Even though they know exactly how to get each other off, they take extra time, they experiment, they still surprise each other sexually. Afterward, they fire things up and head out, on the road of life and love together, stopping at Denny's to fuel their appetites, which are still plenty strong.

IAN: *I like this scenario. Not just the sex part, but the idea that not only will I be able to afford college tuition in the year 2025, but that I'll have a pimped out new euro-van to go along with it. Now that turns me on.*

HEIDI: *No kidding! Here's to a lifetime of rockin' vans and knockin' knees. Cheers!*

IAN: *Cheers!*

In this Time of Colic it's easy to feel as if our kids will never be grown, that we'll never have adult fun. The good news is that time does pass—too quickly! Parenting is remarkable that way; some days seem just endless, and yet, blink—and another year has gone by. So fear not, before you know it, you'll be shut out and dealing with a surly teenager who wants nothing to do with you. Does that mean you should wait for that to happen? Heck, no. Now's the time to get it on again, and set the foundation for a life of getting it on. While we agree that it does get better as the kids get older, it's dangerous to count on that. It's too easy to not look at and talk about real issues and say, "Oh, well, we'll figure it out when the kids are in college," because honestly, by that time too much might have built up or been left unsaid. You don't want to wake up twenty years from now and realize how far apart you've grown. You don't want to just be co-parents of young children, you want to have fun together, right now, in this imperfect, exhausted, sexually challenging moment. And, sure, what the little one needs right now is a mouth full of warm breast milk, but what she'll need down the road is a stable home, and happy parents who are still deeply connected to each other.

As we've seen—and as most of you already know—maintaining that connection is not an easy task. Life is happy to get in the way; to gang up with hormones and body blues, to hitch trains with conflict and control issues to derail things. But you don't have to let it. Decide not to choose between hotness and harmony. Or between fucking and family. You can have it all, a beautiful compromise of sex and stability. Of course you will have ups and downs, dry spells and wet (!) spells. But hopefully, you now know a little more how to talk about it together. Hopefully now you know you're not alone in this, you're not weird or over-sexed or prudish. You are, in fact, each simply human, with your own individual traps, trip-ups, and quirks challenging you to overcome them, to use them, to share them, and what do you know, to enjoy them again and again with each other.

A BEAUTIFUL COMPROMISE: WHAT WE WANT YOU TO KNOW
You're Not Alone

Right now tens of millions of Americans (most of them parents, many of them new parents) are stuck in a sex rut—one that has lasted days, weeks, months, even years. That's right, years. People in slumps start to live lives of quiet desperation and wait way too long before finally dealing with the issue. Like a baseball player who gets into a slump, the psychology behind a dry spell is often pernicious. You may not hear booing from the stands, but, too often, you boo yourself. If you internalize the feeling of being a loser in love, it becomes a self-fulfilling prophecy. So if you're stuck in a slump, stop beating yourself up and get back in the game. Sometimes we think an issue or problem is obvious and out in the open when, in fact, our partner has no idea what we're really feeling or thinking, or the extent to which we're feeling it. Maybe you're lying in bed next to your partner and feeling a million miles apart. But you're only one little touch away. Get your tongues wagging, but remember, when it comes to sex, a whisper sometimes is perceived as a roar.

> My husband and I find that we never seem to be able to get it together for sex—we are either too tired, there's a little one in our bed (we have a 3-month-old and a 2-year-old), or one of us isn't in the mood. I kind of feel that this is part of being parents to young kids—that things will improve as they get older. What's wrong with that?
>
> —FIONA, 32

DEAR (SEX) DIARY:

MONDAY:

blah day, no sex /no time

TUESDAY:

Irritated, no sex/watch TV instead

WEDNESDAY:

fighting fighting fighting no sex/too mad

THURSDAY:

I feel fat. No sex/not worth it

FRIDAY:

What's wrong with me? No sex/too tired

SATURDAY:

What's wrong with US? No sex/still too tired

SUNDAY:

everything sucks, no sex/tried, baby woke up

MONDAY:

Everything is right in the world sex/good sex, great sex

It's Not Always Easy

Okay. In the introduction to this book we asked you to take a chance and dive in to this. We asked you to start the work. And that's what it can feel like sometimes, work. But that doesn't mean it's not right. Too often we're sold a bill of goods that says we'll be happy and sexually fulfilled forever if we just end up with the right Mr. or Mrs., but that's just not true. And many of us children of divorce don't have role models to show us another way. We want our fairy tale, dang it. But fairy tales lack something pretty important: They're not real. Reality may not be pretty or sexy all the time, but it's real, it's honest and authentic—and priceless in its own way.

History, Herstory, Your Story Continues

Our sexual history isn't just something that happened in the past. It's something that's happening right now. Your sexual history is so much more than just the number of partners you've had. It's who you are and what you bring to those experiences. It's how you value your sexual identity and the expression, gratification, and growth of that identity. Your sexual history is the sense of self-esteem and self-respect you bring to your sex life. And it's never too late to change it, to work on it. It's never too late to take ownership of your sexuality and allow yourself to truly become a "sexual person."

Being a sexual person means that you're willing and able to communicate proactively about sexual issues with your partner, that you're committed to the spirit of ongoing sexual creativity, that you sustain your sexual fitness and live a sexually healthy life. Being a sexual person means that you're tuned in and turned on rather than tuned out and turned off, and that you're comfortable with your fantasies. It also means that you're aware of past experiences that may be impairing your full enjoyment of sex, that you have empathy for your partner and his or her issues, that you recognize that sexual desire ebbs and flows across the life cycle (both within yourself and within your relationship), and that sex changes. As do people. And relationships. That's what keeps it all so fun.

It's also time to start thinking about the sexual history you're creating for your own growing family. As we've seen in Chapter 7, the sexual environment kids grow up in can have a lasting impact. And so can the relationships they're watching. (Yes, folks, they're watching. And listening. To everything!) It's good to explore these as parents, as we try to navigate questions about birds and bees with our own kids. Parents often email us asking, "How do we talk to our kids about sex?" "My son wants to know where babies come from, and why he doesn't have a vagina." The questions never stop coming. As our little ones grow up, we tend to try to avoid the issues more than deal with them, and cross our fingers and hope they'll become healthy adults who won't need to read the revised edition of this book when they're dealing with parenting your grandchildren. One of the most important things you can give your children is a healthy, happy model of what it means to be in an intimate, loving relationship.

It's Worth It

Over time a sex-starved relationship leads to a disconnected, unloving relationship, and the whole thing collapses. Sex is at the heart of parents staying connected and contented and creating a happy healthy home for the kids. Parents who have sex are better parents because they're happier, healthier, more affectionate, fight less, and don't sweat so much of the small stuff. Marriage is better with sex. There's no way around it, it just is. And, for some of us, life is better with marriage. Maybe, in a million years people will look back and laugh, *Remember when people were MONOGAMOUS? That's so 2010.* But for now, some of us dig it. Some of us think that long-term sex looks pretty darn good. One study of marital satisfaction at Penn University and the University of Lincoln-Penn tracked two thousand married people over a seventeen-year period and found that marital satisfaction declined precipitously in the first ten years of marriage. (Hmmm—wonder what generally happens in the first ten years of marriage—oh yeah . . . kids.) But there are people who defy the statistics and manage to stay married and happy over the long term and actually still feel passion for their partners. This is what we aspire toward: to be the exception to the rule, to be exceptional, to continue to see life, and our partners, through the rose-tinted glasses of romantic life. To stay infatuated—with our partners, our relationships, our lives.

IN CONCLUSION

Now, more than ever, we need to turn off the noise and tune in to our authentic sexual selves as people, parents, and lovers. We need to reclaim our innate erotic potential and rediscover our ability to live vitally and passionately. You only have one life, and you deserve to live it to the fullest. Yes, having kids makes it hard to remember that passion and fullness, but having good sex can be a beautiful reminder. Domesticity and hot sex don't have to be mutually exclusive, though there's no doubt that balancing love, marriage, and the baby carriage is a complicated act. As Ian said in the Introduction, this is all about putting the oxygen mask on us first; we've got to take care of ourselves, as adults, in order to take care of the kids. This is probably some of the funnest stuff you can do "for the sake of the kids." You know what to do, folks—it! It's time for us to send you on your way to a happy sexual life, to go forth and prosper. And propagate.

So go on, get on it. And get it on again.

Since You Asked:
Your Questions Answered

In my mom's group the women always talk about their lack of libido—I feel like a freak. MY libido is fine`... better than ever, actually. But what about when it's the woman who wants sex—and the guy who is always "too tired"?

HEIDI: Looking back to when my first daughter was young, I was definitely the one with the missing libido. But now, seven years and another baby later (what was I thinking!?), I've noticed how our roles have changed. While JB's libido is still generally higher than mine, his seems to have gone down some and mine has gone up. More often than not, I'm the one initiating sex these days. Similarly, I used to be the one begging for him to share his feelings with me, but these days I've been taking on more of the traditional guy role—too often I hear myself saying, "I don't want to talk about it." Even in bed, our roles have changed; JB often wants to reach out to me and "make sweet love," while I often just want to get fucked! Maybe it's because I'm so darn busy these days, or maybe because all the hormones and pregnancies have shifted things around so much. Who knows? But either way, the point of all this over-sharing? It's to remind you that relationships in and out of bed aren't static, they're always changing and evolving—for the good and the bad and the just plain confusing. So don't be afraid to break out of the structure we've set up and glean what works best for you and yours. Maybe you identify with the "dad" points in some of the chapters and the "mom" points in others. It's all good. As long as it's working toward the greater good—of having great sex again.

You're frightening me. My wife and I are trying to start a family. And she's the hottest woman ever to walk the earth. I'd hate to think that sex will be so darn hard after we have a baby!

IAN: According to eminent marriage therapist John Gottman, 67 percent of couples have a precipitous drop in relationship happiness in the first three years of their first baby's life. It's unfortunate that this amazing time comes with that kind of baggage. But then again, growth is often uncomfortable—and that's what new families are doing—growing, as individuals and as a couple. But that doesn't mean it's not good for you.

HEIDI: And hey, don't worry; JB still thinks I'm the hottest woman to ever walk the earth. I mean, I think he hit on me in the hospital room minutes after my C-section! My robe was open or something . . . Now, I'm often just the "hot, unattainable" woman walking the earth, or pacing the halls, at midnight, with a fussy baby. Yes, figuring this stuff out is hard. Things might not fall apart or slow down for you. But why not start talking about the what-ifs right now? Why not jump in and get proactive, since you're no longer getting prophylactic?

I'm not feeling like a sex goddess these days, and my husband takes it so personally. What's his problem? It's not him, it's me.

IAN: Speaking for the guys, I love this point—not because you don't feel like the sex goddess you once used to feel like, but because you're saying it's not our fault. Rationally, we know it's not us, but you know sex isn't wired into the rational part of our brain—sexual arousal comes from primitive reptile parts of the brain, the amygdala, which is also wired into our fight or flight response. This fight or flight response is designed to help us make snap decisions, like whether to shake hands with that guy walking up to us, or to deck him one. We're thinking friend or foe. So when you rebuff our sexual advances, it immediately bypasses our rational prefrontal cortex and goes straight to that primitive response. So, please baby please (of course that's the title of a book I was just reading to Beckett), keep letting us know that it's not our fault, that you really do still think we're cute and sexy and manly, and also know that when you rebuff us there might be a snap response that we can't help (not that that's an excuse), but we may need a few moments to get rational.

HEIDI: That darn reptile brain! But I guess that does make sense.

Here's another way of thinking about it. As I mentioned in my first book, I always got kind of pissy when JB acted all "blue" on me after I put him off, until he explained it like this: "I'm sorry, babe, I was just really excited to screw. And now it's hard for me to lie next to you. I'm going to grab some string cheese, watch Sports Center, and cool down. You're welcome to join me, but if you don't, I want you to know I'm not angry or trying to punish you by leaving the room. I just have a very bad headache—in my penis." Now that makes sense to the part of my brain otherwise possibly reserved for "hurt feelings/panic about relationship status."

IAN: When you say JB acted all blue on you, don't you really mean he got "all blue balls" on you? This is the discomfort men feel in the testicles when the blood-filled genital area is not relieved by orgasm. The correct term for blue balls is epididymitis, an inflammation of the epididymis, which occurs when sperm that have left the testes but not the penis and causes swelling, a bit of a pain, and a bit of bluing due to the pooling of the blood. So maybe JB's balls really do have the blues, metaphorically and literally. But guys aren't the only ones to feel the pain of unrelieved sexual tension. Many women often feel a heaviness in the pelvic area and a lingering sense of ache. Maybe the condition should be called "blue vulva."

HEIDI: That sounds like a David Lynch movie! And here I thought he just meant it figuratively "hurt" him when I lead him on. Thanks for the heads up on that, Ian.

OK, I'll just say it. I'm freaked out by my wife's breasts. She wanted me to kiss them and I was afraid of getting sprayed! Am I uptight?

IAN: While some guys are really into the idea of getting a sip of breast milk (there's actually a whole porn industry based on lactating moms!), some guys want to stay away from the spray as much as possible. I happen to be in the latter category. I've always been really attracted to Lisa's natural breast size and found the whole metamorphosis a little disconcerting—I didn't find them as sexy on her as everyone else seemed to find them. Maybe I just knew on some internal level that they weren't mine anymore (for the time being at least).

HEIDI: I'm right there with you. I've never enjoyed being part of the "bigger the better the tighter the sweater" club. They hurt my back, people stare—I used to enjoy jogging, but now that's out of the question. I'm worried about knocking out innocent bystanders with these unwieldly kazongas. I'm like a giant boob ogre! Mwwhhahaha. Recently I even had to threaten a male friend that I was going to replace the cream in his White Russian with breast milk if he didn't stop ogling. But it's really not his fault; my girlfriends are in awe of these bad girls of mine too. Maybe I should look into that lactating porn thing . . . as least I could make some money off these suckers. (No pun intended!)

Have either of you ever thought seriously about swinging?

HEIDI: Ah, monogamy. The work of it. The comfy underwear. The grueling weeklong fights. The unflinching honesty about things like smelly body parts and bad haircuts. Why on Earth do we do this to ourselves? For JB and me, the question isn't really

"Why monogamy?" It's "Why not anything else?" Why not swing? Because, honestly, we think we would hate it. Because we'd want it to be fun, but really it would be just another thing to turn us into a big mess. The truth is, for some folks, it's entirely possible that looking outside the familiar strictly for sex may be a good choice—though we hesitate to call it natural. After all, in the "natural" world animals do all kinds of nutty things. Some are monogamous, lots are not. And a few eat the heads of their partners after mating. That doesn't mean that it's right for everyone.

Beyond that, me swinging would be like being an alcoholic working in a bar. I tend to fall in love as easily as catching a cold. This is what is "natural" for me: falling prey to the chemical cocktail of dopamine, phenylethylamine, and oxytocin that make me want to give myself over to one person and lose myself in love. The last time I did that I ended up here, in this perhaps unnatural, often challenging, place called marriage. The drugs may have worn off some, but I'm still happy to be here—still stoned on the safety and comfort it offers me. Do we ever think about stepping out of our "vanilla" ways and spicing things up? Sure. In a perfect world, JB would go to bed each night with me and my stripper girlfriends. But do we seriously consider it? Nope. The truth is, I don't do well separating sex and love. I don't like sex with no strings attached. For me, good sex is all about the strings—the sticky, slippery, confining, liberating strings of emotion. That's what turns me on. Monogamy is a beautiful compromise. In exchange for working our asses off at this monogamy thing, in exchange for passing up the excitement of sex with other people, we get something else. We get to eliminate one variable. We get to look at the hard stuff without the distraction of the easy always being an option. We get to make new mistakes instead of getting stuck at our same old places, our same old jumping off points. It is hard, but it's also deep—not unlike the sex we've been having lately, yet another payoff.

IAN: This is a question we all probably explore at some point. I mean, does monogamy really make sense, or are we all just avoiding the simple truth that, when looking at the forest for the trees, we're pretty much alone amongst other animals. Nature tends to be about 99 percent of the sluttish type, excluding a few holdouts: prairie voles (basically little gerbil-sized rats), pygmy marmosets (basically the smallest living monkey), gray foxes, gray-headed albatrosses, and a few others. So, seriously, who are we kidding? If we want to stay faithful but still be enlivened with all that is eros, it's going to take a hell of a lot more than date night. Makes sense when you consider that studies have shown that couples in long-term relationships tend to feel less content and satisfied. But as we said in the Conclusion, there are those who not only make long-term love work, but who make it work well. I'm hoping to be one of those.

I stretched a lot in childbirth. I hate the way I look down there now, and worry my husband can't feel anything. Isn't there something I can do about this?

IAN: The real culprit of "too looseness" is often the tone of a woman's pelvic floor muscles. While most women find that things get more or less back to normal three to six months after birth, some might have more damage, depending on the size of their babies, the number of births, and of course, Kegels. (Yes, I know, it's as tedious as flossing, but like flossing, has a real payoff. Beyond that, you can do them when you're actually having sex—it's fun, and then, you're done). Recent research also hints that the long-term tone of your pelvic floor muscles may ultimately have more to do with your heredity than vaginal birthing.

HEIDI: Someone emailed me asking about plastic surgery for her vagina because she was "disfigured" from her son's birth. Yikes. That doesn't seem right to me. I mean, I'm no doctor (though I like to play one with my man sometimes), but that seems excessive.

IAN: It's called vaginal rejuvenation surgery. It's a procedure that used to be reserved for serious problems like congenital malformations, incontinence, or serious injuries related to childbirth. Now, it's something women can do in an outpatient clinic if they have enough money and don't feel their precious bits are up to standard for one reason or another. If a loose vagina is bothering you—for you—then by all means let's fix that. Talk to your medical caregiver about tools (or toys!) that can help you do your Kegels more efficiently, or ask if she can refer you to a physiotherapist. In the meantime, make sex more enjoyable as is—try using a small vibrator inside you at the same time your partner is, or use your hands to add pressure and sensation.

HEIDI: Yes—I'm all for a woman doing what she needs to do to feel good about herself in and out of bed, but it should be for herself, not because she's worried about someone else's pleasure. It's another wrinkle in the perfect, rather than real, mother phenomena. Perfect mothers bear children with no scars or physical changes, perfect mothers look youthful and energized, perfect mothers don't age, get wrinkled, or wear ugly sweatpants because they're too tired to get dressed. Perfect mothers have tight, perky vaginas to give their husbands maximum pleasure—never mind that for most of us the clitoris is where our pleasure is really at.

IAN: That's right. If you've tried everything else and your doctor recommends it, surgery may indeed be the right choice. But it should be the last choice, not the quick-fix first one, and not one because you're uptight about your imperfections or afraid you look like Frankengina. Of course, if things continue to "not feel right" after your six-week checkup, don't let it go unchecked.

HEIDI: Maybe we're supposed to be a little looser after childbirth. Maybe it allows us to stretch and get deeper into things with our partner, deeper into our appreciation of our bodies and deeper into embracing our imperfections. Because as freaky as it is to feel like things aren't the way they were before motherhood, more freaky is the idea that it doesn't change us at all.

Why does my husband seem to be thinking about sex every second of the day, and it feels like I can go days without having nary a sexual thought? Even just thinking about sex can feel like another chore!

IAN: So I walked around the Thompson Street playground in New York City, asking moms and dads how much they'd thought about sex in the last hour (no, they didn't think I was a perv, I had my doctor glasses on). Guess what? No surprise—almost every guy had thought about sex at least once, whereas almost every woman had thought about it not at all. For guys, thinking about sex is wired into the neural pathways of our mindscapes, wherever we happen to be. It definitely is not a chore. Not always with women, who have to work at it more. But just letting yourself breathe for a moment to take in the eros that throbs and pulses all around you and letting yourself have a sexy thought is something you should put for sure on the to-do list. And pretty soon it won't feel like a chore.

HEIDI: Sorry Ian, but you make it sound so simple. For some of us it's more than just not getting to the desire stage—for some of us the sexy thoughts don't even happen . . . at least not without some work.

IAN: Hmm. You just got me thinking about something.

HEIDI: Wait, let me guess . . . it got you thinking about sex! Because you're a *guy!*

IAN: Nice one. But seriously . . . okay. It did. But it's not just that we're thinking about sex. It's that the "thinking about" part of it is actually wired into our wanting system. We don't just see something sexy and think to ourselves, "Oh that swimsuit model on the cover of Sports Illustrated is really sexy," and that's that. A little neural impulse shoots straight down from our brain to our penises, and we're overtaken with a sudden jolt of sexual craving. In this sense, men really do think (not to mention see, hear, smell, and taste) with our penises. Desire and arousal are incredibly interlinked; show us something sexy and in no time at all we're ready to have sex. So when you talk about missing the wanting to have sex, but not actually missing the having it part, I wonder if you're really getting at a fundamental difference in how men and women are sexually wired.

HEIDI: That's why Viagra is such a success story with men, while female Viagra was pretty much a bust. Give a guy an erection, and he wants to use it. Not so with us ladies. Let's be honest, we all know Viagra for women that really worked would have to come with a kit including coupons for things like therapy and housecleaning. I also just don't perceive things to have "sexy potential" in the same way JB might. I mean, he can see a rug and think: "I could have sex on that rug." I see a rug and think, "rug," or more accurately, "dirty rug," or, "rug filled with choking hazards." It takes a lot more than seeing something to get my thoughts going and a whole lot more than that to actually get me physically in the mood.

IAN: I think this calls for yet another Esther Perel quote from her book *Mating in Captivity:* "The sensuality that women experience with their children is, in some ways, much more in keeping with female sensuality in general. For women, much more than for men, sexuality exists along what the Italian historian Francesco Alberoni calls a principle of continuity. Female eroticism is diffuse, not localized in the genitals, but distributed throughout the body, mind, and senses. It is tactile and auditory, linked to smell, skin, and contact; arousal is often more subjective than physical, and desire arises on a lattice of emotion."

HEIDI: Oooh, she's good! I like "lattice of emotion." My lattice is too often overrun by the weeds and ivy of life, like that quick-spreading negativity and the ever hardy saying yes to stuff I really should have said no to. Even climbing vines with beautiful flowers can smother when not kept in check—how's desire supposed to peak its way out? What are we sacrificing for the *Better Homes and Gardens* garden? For many of us, it's time to haul out the big loppers. It's prunin' time!

I keep dreaming about other women. Does this mean I'm a bad husband? I love my wife—but these dreams are ca-razy.

IAN: While a lot of fantasy takes place while awake, whether during a particularly boring meeting at work or compliments of the Internet, our deepest sexual longings also find their way into our dreams. Sleep puts the brain on autopilot and allows the deeper desires inside of us to come out and play. As neuroscientist Mark Solms, a leading expert in the field of sleep research, explains: "Dreaming does for the brain what Saturday morning cartoons do for the kids: It keeps them sufficiently entertained so that the serious players in the household can get needed recovery time. Without such diversion, the brain would be urging us up and out into the world to keep it fully engaged."

What are the majority of us dreaming about? A recent study by researchers David B. King and Teresa DeCicco at Trent University in Peterborough, Ontario, found that intercourse is the most common sexual behavior in dreams. A healthy 37 percent of participants reported having a sexual dream once a week, while a staggering 19 percent reported sex dreams up to five times per week! Interestingly, those who reported higher sexual satisfaction in their relationships tended to dream more often about their partner. Seventy-two percent of participants believed their sex dreams had meaning and 49 percent gained further insight into their waking relationships, past, present, or potential.

So, what does this tell us? That sexual fantasies are completely normal and also help us understand what's going on in our waking lives. Too many of us feel guilty about our fantasy life, whether because we dream about someone other than our current partner or because our imagination runs wild with behavior we would never condone in real life.

Dreams free the brain to explore secret, extraordinary realms without the obligations of everyday life. Practicality, morality, and logic don't apply. Flooded by a barrage of images, memories, and thoughts, you can basically kick back and enjoy the show. So, whatever dreams may come, enjoy them, try to learn from them, and don't worry if they take you to bizarre or unfamiliar places. Many of us feel unnerved by our own fantasies, and all of us have comfort zones in terms of how far we will let our imaginations wander. At first blush, our fantasies often seem to sit in stark contrast to the moral and societal values with which we were raised. For this reason, we tend to self-censor and repress them instead of letting our fantasies breathe and flourish.

I have three kids, C-section scars, and a belly that won't quit. Why is my husband is still buying me stripper lingerie?

HEIDI: Yeah, guys. About that lingerie: Tight, show-everything fancies might tickle yours, but they can leave us feeling a little hippo-in-the-hammock. Leave the prickly gear for pornos and porcupines. I recently came across a statistic that said something like 75 percent of men end up buying their ladies lingerie for Valentine's Day, but less than 10 percent of women actually want their guys to buy them lingerie. So what's the deal, Ian?

IAN: Speaking as a guy who has bought my fair share of lingerie for Lisa, much of which has gone unworn, we often buy it for perfectly good reasons: to be intimate, personal, naughty, sexy—to recognize that underneath it all we still recognize or yearn for the naughty sexual vixen that resides within you. Sometimes we buy lingerie that actually embodies (in your body) a little bit of unconscious, or not so unconscious code for an aspect of sex we're looking for, a provocation to turn our bedroom into a playroom. Buying you ridiculous lingerie is our little bit of sexual optimism. It's about breaking out of our usual roles and reclaiming something sexy and secret that's only between the two of us. That's what we're trying to do by buying this stuff.

HEIDI: Aww. That's sweet. Okay, you can buy 'em, but that doesn't mean we're going to wear 'em. How about we meet in the middle? Something slightly more modest and significantly more comfy—negligees that show off breasts but cover the belly and butt and hit mid-thigh, leaving the details of what's to come to your (and our) imagination. That way we can uncover what we want as we go; let us hike it up and take it off as part of the slippery, silky fun.

What exactly is a sex therapist, how do I know if I need one, and where can I find a sex therapist that's qualified to work with me?

IAN: Unlike many other mental health professions, sex therapy is a largely unregulated field that does not require licensure in most states. As a result, there are lots of people who call themselves sex therapists who are largely unqualified to practice. A sex therapist is very often someone who was originally trained in a related field such as psychology, social work, or counseling and has chosen to go on to specialize in the treatment of sexual issues. A sex therapist might also be a person who did not previously come from a related clinical field, but has received both a proper education, as well as clinical supervision, from a university that offers a qualified graduate program in human sexuality.

When dealing with sex and relationships, it's often difficult to separate the sex part from the relationship part. But that's exactly what a sex therapist tries to do—not that sex therapists don't care about your bigger relationship concerns, or don't want to talk about them, but very often it's important to isolate the actual sexual issues from the underlying relationship factors. Experience has shown that fixing your relationship won't necessarily fix your sex life, so sex therapists like to focus on specific behavioral therapies that are known to successfully address a broad range of sexual problems.

Some of the more common problems that sex therapists deal with include premature ejaculation, erectile disorder, female orgasmic dysfunction (inability to reach orgasm), female sexual unresponsiveness, low libido and lack of desire, interpersonal psychodynamics around sexual issues, and lack of communication between couples about their sex lives.

HEIDI: Oh. So, it's not going to be like the sex therapist on HBO's *Real Sex*?

IAN: Uh—no. This reminds me of a time I was running late for a session with a newly married couple and when I finally walked through the door, they were both sitting on the couch completely naked, nervously covering their private parts. When I asked them why they were undressed, the husband said, "Isn't this sex therapy? Aren't you going to watch us have sex and then give us tips and pointers?" I explained that sex therapy was talk therapy and all homework assignments would be done outside the office. I thought they'd be relieved when I told them to get dressed, but they were disappointed. Turns out, they were looking forward to getting it on while someone else was watching.

HEIDI: Well, there you go—I guess there's a little bit of the exhibitionist in everyone.

IAN: If you go to a sex therapist, you will not be asked to get undressed or engage in sexual activity. Sex therapists use their time with patients to foster communication and understanding, as well as to pinpoint the precise nature of a given sexual problem.

Sex therapists will often give their patients "homework" that includes intimacy-building activities of a sexual nature and then discuss the results of those assignments later during an in-office session. Sexual dissatisfaction is the number two reason for divorce in this country and, unfortunately, lawyers far outnumber sex therapists. But if you're having a sexual problem and would like help, you can locate a qualified sex therapist by contacting organizations such as AASECT (the American Association of Sex Educators Counselors and Therapists), www.aasect.org, and the American Board of Sexology, www.americanboardofsexology.com, or the American Association for Marriage and Family Therapy, www.aamft.org.

My wife thinks sex is dirty—she thinks good girls don't do "bad" things.

HEIDI: As we've seen, being in a relationship can bring up issues from childhood. Some of us have some minor sexual hang-ups, some of us have big ones, and many of us have regular old hang-ups that get in the way of letting go and enjoying sex.

IAN: In Dr. Aline Zoklbrod's thoughtful book *Sex Smart*, she examines how childhood shapes one's adult sexual life, and she divides home environments into the seven following types based on how sexual topics are handled.[1] While these types are not set in stone, it's good to see where you fit. It's time to get rid of all our sexual baggage and start keeping our own shared storage shed.

- **The Ideal Environment**: In this happy home, sexual curiosity is encouraged, questions about sex are answered with age-appropriate information, and privacy and independence are respected and actively cultivated.
- **The Predominantly Nurturing Environment**: This environment is similar to the Ideal Environment above, albeit with some glaring gaps. For instance, a parent or sibling suffers from intermittent periods of depression or illness, or a divorce and remarriage cause a break in the seamless functioning of the Ideal Environment.
- **The Evasive Environment**: In this scenario, the parents generally avoid the subject of sex and foster an environment where asking about sexual matters is uncomfortable. This is often consistent with a family where the

[1] Dr. Zoklbrod bases her typology on previous work published by Bolton, F., L. Morris, and A. MacEachron. *Males at Risk: The Other Side of Child Sexual Abuse*. Newbury Park, Calif.: Sage Publications, Inc., 1989.

parents are not openly affectionate with each other, even if they are affectionate to their children.

- **The Permissive Environment**: At the other end of the pendulum is the home where sex is discussed too openly, with parents providing too much information too soon. In such a home, parents generally share intimate information with their children about their own sex lives and actively encourage their children to experiment sexually at too young an age to appreciate the emotional and psychological consequences.
- **The Negative Environment**: In such a home, non-marital sex is not merely avoided but treated as immoral, providing a fertile nesting ground for homophobia, misogyny, and sexual problems in later life, including fear of masturbation, inability to achieve orgasm in women, and premature ejaculation in men.
- **The Seductive Environment**: In this scenario, relationships between parents and children or siblings are not overtly sexual, but are tinged with an inappropriate level of sexuality, including the routine discussion of age-inappropriate sexual matters.
- **The Overtly Sexual Environment, or Abusive Environment**: This environment is characterized by inappropriate sexual contact between a parent and child. Just to be absolutely clear, this inappropriate contact does constitute sexual abuse, even if the child often doesn't recognize it as such, or blocks it out. Whether the abuse happens just once or occurs over an extended period, is

inflicted by a member of the immediate family or
extended family of friends and relatives, growing up in
an overtly sexual home can inflict long-term damage
that impedes the ability to engage in healthy adult
sexual relationships.

Growing up in an overtly sexual environment is just
one of the ways children experience sexual trauma. People
who grew up in abusive environments, which may not
have necessarily been sexually abusive, often experience
anxiety, lack of trust, fear of touch, and other symptoms
that affect their adult intimate relationships. Every year,
millions of children in the United States are the victims of
either direct or indirect domestic violence and have been
hurt by a parent or watched a parent get hurt.

If you're in this situation, it's extremely likely that you
might not have thought about the connection between
the nonsexual trauma you may have experienced as a
child and the sexual intimacy issues you may be dealing
with in your adult relationships. Many people who suffer
from sex addiction, or conversely have no sexual desire,
often find that they came from backgrounds that inspired
fear and anxiety in relation to intimacy. The relationships
they witnessed around them inspired distrust and unease
rather than comfort and security. Many people are not on
the extreme ends of the spectrum but have difficulties
with intimacy nonetheless. Other traumas, such as a
sexual assault or rape or a nonsexual assault that occurred
outside the home during childhood, can also create

lifelong intimacy issues unless they were properly
addressed with parental support, understanding, and
family and individual therapy.

In the case of serious traumas, treatment simply falls
outside the purview of this book, and I would recommend you see a qualified therapist. Consider this as a
starting point for talking to a professional and discussing your issues openly with your partner.

**The other night my wife was too tired for sex so I offered
to go down on her. She said she wasn't in the mood. It
was too much work! What the . . . work? I'd take that "job"
any day of the week! Why can't she just lay back and enjoy
herself?**

IAN: This reminds me of a chapter I wrote in *She Comes First*
titled "The Cunnilinguist Manifesto," which was a bit of a
piss-take on Marx's Communist Manifesto: "From each according to their abilities, to each according to their needs." That whole
rap. My version is: "To her according to your abilities, from you
according to her needs."

Easier said than done. Especially after the birth of a child. A
new mom may be deeply conflicted when it comes to receiving
oral sex, and the experience may be fraught with anxiety. There's
an utter nakedness to oral sex—a vulnerability that we need to
respect and honor. She is exposing herself to be seen, smelled,
tasted, and observed firsthand; she is permitting the exploration
of a part of her body that she herself may find newly unfamiliar

and mysterious. Only by inspiring trust will you lull her into a deeper, more instinctive zone of the self, a place where she can shed all inhibition and surrender herself.

HEIDI: Hold on, mister! You may be all down with going down, but I know for a fact—because I asked him—that if we had a life-like model of a vulva that looked, tasted, smelled, and felt like a real one, JB wouldn't just hang out there mauwing on it all day just for fun. He doesn't have any problem getting intimate with my sexy bits, but let's be honest—it's the getting me off part that's fun for him, not my glorious me-ness. Since oral sex was off limits for me during pregnancy due to certain changes in taste and smell (and the fact that JB felt weird being so "face to face" with the little one), I was nervous about bringing it up again post-baby. When he offered, I felt put on the spot, but later, as things got more heated it worked its way right in to the natural flow of things. I was shy . . . until I saw how excited he was to see (and taste and feel . . .) my excitement again.

I know this isn't cool, but how can I tell my husband I don't like the stuff he does in bed?

IAN: You can start by making talking about sex sexy. It's not enough to just be positive and constructive, but to actually talk about the sex you want in a way that inspires a guy to want it too—let's say he's not so generous when it comes to lavishing you with oral attention, or his idea of foreplay is a peck on the lips and a hand down your pants. Tell him about what you want in the form of a sexy thought or a sexy dream. Say, "Hey you, I don't know what my unconscious was thinking last night, but I had a really sexy dream about you." Trust me, he'll be interested and want to know more. And then go on to describe the sex you'd like to be having rather than focusing on the sex you're not having—make sense?

HEIDI: I think that makes sexy sense! You can also watch naughty movies together or read books. When you see or read something you think you might like to try, point it out. Say, "Wow, that looks kinda fun. . . ." Then make a move to show you mean business.

My little one is obsessed with his penis. He keeps asking about the birds and bees. Is this normal? What should I tell him? I can only stall so long.

HEIDI: I know plenty of guys who are still obsessed with their penises! This stuff is hard. My oldest girl is a little precocious, so I've been through the ringer on this one. Most recently, I was driving her home from school when she wanted to know how our friends—two moms—made a baby. At the time, I wasn't worried—after all, I was a sex columnist—and the growing bump of baby number two had already sparked many good conversations about baby making. Heck, I was proud her logical little six-year-old mind knew a man's sperm needed to be involved somehow. That is until the basic rundown on sperm banks I gave her wasn't enough. Until she wanted real details.

"Well," she said, "then what do they do with the sperm?"

Trying to be as straightforward but simple as I could, I told her they put it up a woman's vagina where it meets an egg and makes a baby. In the rearview mirror I could see her scowl.

"But you and daddy didn't do that, did you?" she said, shocked, eyeing my belly.

"Sure we did," I said, a little put off by her tone.

"But how, Mom? How did you get the sperm up there?" She was still scowling back there, frustrated that she didn't understand.

I took a breath, pulled up to the light and gave her the goods: "With Daddy's penis."

"Oh."

I took another breath. Honestly, I was happy for her silence, thinking I'd done pretty good but also feeling like I was ready to talk about something else.

"Oh. So . . ." she starts—and I knew I was in for more—"So, it's like putting a hot dog in a bun."

I wanted to laugh. Until I turned around to look at her. I could see her wheels turning. She knows how to put a hot dog in a bun. She likes putting hot dogs in buns. Hot dogs in buns are fun.

"Does it hurt?"

Hoo boy. I took a second, when I should have maybe taken five, and explained that no, it doesn't hurt that it's something grown-ups actually kind of like to do, emphasizing the grown-ups part. And then I instantly regretted it. The look on her face as we pulled up to the house told me what was coming.

"So, then . . . can kids do it?"

I turned around and looked at her. It was obvious she was envisioning potential hot dog/bun sharing mates and encounters: her cousins, the neighbor, her best friend. Suddenly, I wasn't sex-positive mom anymore. I wasn't a sex columnist. I was just a hormonal, protective mother bear. I helped her out of her booster, and put my arm around her.

"Nope," I said breezily, "Oh no. We don't share germs, remember?"

Okay, so maybe I wasn't totally clean on that. Maybe I took an easy way out. Maybe, I panicked—because while I don't want to inhibit my daughter or have her think of sex as dirty, I do want her to be smart about it, to be careful and well, dare I say, "make good choices." Or maybe, like all of us parents, it was the best I could give at the time. Maybe next time I'll get it just right, I'll hit it out of the park. But for now at least I know she's getting her information, for what it's worth, from me. And I have a hunch that this isn't the last time we'll be talking about the ins and outs of hot dogs and buns.

It's taken almost ten years after kid number two to regain my naughtiness, and now my first kid's aware enough to know when hanky-panky is in the air, so circumspection's always in order! How do I work that out?

As for older kids knowing hanky-panky is in the air, we say—good! Get a good lock and set some ground rules about knocking and privacy. Take advantage of Saturday.morning cartoons and say you're sleeping in together. Head for the shower and tell them you're saving water by showering together. Certainly they don't need to know the details of what's going on, but it's fine for them to know that Mom and Dad need special time too. They won't know whether you're doing hanky-panky or hokeypokey in there, but they will know that you're doing it together. And that's what it's all about.

Acknowledgments

IAN'S SHOUT-OUTS

Thanks to:

Heidi, for putting a bug in my ear, and being the best collaborator and co-writer a guy could ask for.

Richard Abate, my agent, friend, good sport, and returner of phone calls.

Owen and Beckett, this project truly couldn't have happened without you and nearly didn't because of you: You keep the days bustling, the nights busy, and the mornings bleary.

Lisa, for not giving up me. (I think I said that in the last book, too. How do you put up with me?)

My mother, it wasn't easy, here we are—I couldn't be anywhere without you.

My grandmother Jean, for her will to power (and love).

My father, amidst it all.

The memory of my cantankerous beast, Houdini—my one-and-only dog-boy.

My friends and family, old and new—we live and love through it all.

HEIDI'S SHOUT-OUTS

Thanks to:

Ian, for taking on this project, despite your crazy life!

Laura Gross, my agent and friend.

Literarymama.com, for their continued support and inspiration.

My parents, for everything, always.

My friends, for everything, always.

Hector, for being my personal "manny" and a doting grandpa.

JB, as always. You know what you do to me. JUA.

Ramona and Mercy Jean, for putting up with such a cranky, distracted, multi-tasking mom. I love being your mama.

AND FROM BOTH OF US

Thanks to:

Cassie Jones, you're the best! Johnathan Wilber, you're not too bad either!

Mary Ellen O'Neill, for getting this project from the get-go.

Everyone on the Collins team, for their support and warmth.

Special thanks to Jane Black for letting us use her piece "S/M in the Suburbs," which was originally published on www.goodvibrations.com.

Everyone who shared their stories—thank you for letting your voices be heard.